no longer slaves

no longer slaves
set free by Christ

ROY CLEMENTS

inter-varsity press

INTER-VARSITY PRESS
38 De Montfort Street, Leicester LE1 7GP, England

First published 1997

British Library Cataloguing in Publication Data
A catalogue record for this book is available from the British
Library.

ISBN 0–85111–182–3

Set in Garamond No. 3

Typeset in Great Britain by Parker Typesetting Service, Leicester

Printed in Great Britain by Cox & Wyman Ltd, Reading

*Inter-Varsity Press is the book-publishing division of the Universities and
Colleges Christian Fellowship (formerly the Inter-Varsity Fellowship), a
student movement linking Christian Unions in universities and colleges
throughout the United Kingdom and the Republic of Ireland, and a
member movement of the International Fellowship of Evangelical
Students. For information about local and national activities write to
UCCF, 38 De Montfort Street, Leicester LE1 7GP.*

contents

Preface   7

1. An inspired message   9

2. An irrevocable promise   43

3. An inalienable freedom   69

4. An inner war   99

Preface

The strange thing about health is that the more people worry about it the less likely they are to enjoy it. The irony of hypochondria is that quite often it generates real, stress-related illness. A book published some years ago, entitled *The Anatomy of an Illness*, described the key role which laughter can play in strengthening the immune defence system of cancer victims. The evidence seems to suggest that people who can't laugh, because they are inwardly twisted up with anxiety, get sick more often and stay ill longer.

Something rather similar is true of holiness. Some Christians try to achieve it by a strategy of moral and spiritual hypochondria. They build a system of rules and regulations which, if perfectly obeyed, constitutes holiness. Then they spend all their time worried and guilt-ridden over every pedantic detail of it.

The fact is, however, that holiness cannot be achieved in that fashion. At best all that such a legalistic obsession can produce is self-righteousness – which is, ironically, about as far from true Christian holiness as it is possible to get! In reality holiness, like physical health, is the by-product of a life of joyful freedom. It has far more to do with the laughter of the redeemed than with the fear of the slave.

No part of the Bible makes this clearer than the book of Galatians. It is one of the earliest letters that the apostle Paul wrote and it addresses the central issue with which he had to wrestle as a missionary of the early church. What should be the relationship between Gentile Christianity and Judaism? We know from the book of Acts (you can read the story in chapter 15) that certain conservative Jews demanded that Gentile converts should be circumcised, and that Paul adamantly resisted any such requirement. Galatians was written, possibly, soon after the Council in Jerusalem that adjudicated on this debate. In the letter, Paul explains his reasons for this resolute stand.

It comes down to this. Rules can neither save us nor make us holy. Salvation is a gift of God's grace, and holiness is the fruit of his Spirit. We discover both when we are set free from 'the law' by Jesus. Sadly this is a discovery many miss. Trapped in the anxiety-driven web of their spiritual hypochondria, enslaved by a legalistic perfectionism, they fight a losing battle against feelings of failure and worthlessness. They need to learn to laugh! I hope this series of studies, first presented at Word Alive in 1996, may help them to do so.

Cambridge   *Roy Clements*
                                                  12 December 1996

1

An inspired message
Galatians 1 – 2

'Let us never negotiate out of fear, but let us never fear to negotiate.' These wise words from the lips of the late President John F. Kennedy may well be appropriate in the context of the peace talks that continue to limp along in Northern Ireland. In the arena of diplomatic politics, isn't a willingness to negotiate indispensable?

Of course, it would be wrong to surrender to anyone out of cowardice. The terrorist who tries to get his own way by intimidation must never be rewarded. But equally we cannot afford to become so paranoid and defensive that we dare not concede anything. Kennedy put it well.

Intolerance or truth?

One could argue that this same challenge is equally relevant in the area of religious debate. Just think of all the acrimony and bloodshed that have been caused down the years by rigid religious opinions. Painful experience has taught us the value of tolerance. If you want to make a constructive contribution to religious debate, mustn't you express your opinion with modesty, restraint and open-mindedness? As with politics, mustn't there be mental flexibility, and a readiness to negotiate?

> Even if we or an angel from heaven should preach a gospel other than the one we preached to you, let him be eternally condemned! As we have already said, so now I say again: If anybody is preaching to you a gospel other than what you accepted, let him be eternally condemned! (Galatians 1:8–9).

Oh dear! How very unfortunate! Isn't Paul really betraying his old illiberal pharisaical roots here! What a pity? Still, I suppose even great Christians must have their off-days. Could the man who wrote that wonderful chapter about love in his letter to the Corinthians really be as peevishly opinionated as this? Maybe his digestion was playing him up? Or maybe he still had something to learn? Some scholars reckon that Galatians was his very first letter, after all. Better cast a discreet veil of silence over this immoderate language, and say no more about it!

Is that your reaction to these opening lines of Paul's letter to the Galatians – an embarrassing tantrum by a man who should have known better? Some have certainly interpreted it that way. They find Paul's 'abrasive' and 'intolerant' remarks quite out of keeping with Christian charity, and would rather make excuses for him on grounds of sickness or immaturity than suggest there is some positive lesson to be learnt from them.

I want to offer you a contrary evaluation. My suggestion is that far from being a reprehensible display of narrow-mindedness, Paul's words in the opening to his letter actually exemplify a vital principle which no-one needs to grasp more than we do in our pluralist, postmodern, late-twentieth-century environment. The principle is this: *there is such a thing as Truth with a capital T, and that Truth is not negotiable.*

You can negotiate about a Northern Ireland Assembly, about European monetary union, and about the future of Hong Kong. You can negotiate about practically anything in the political sphere, and ought to be willing to do so. There are very few issues over which it is morally right to go to war.

But you cannot negotiate about the Truth.

Our task in this first chapter is to understand why that is so. To do that, we must first briefly introduce the situation to which Paul is writing.

The situation in Galatia

This letter is addressed 'To the churches in Galatia' (1:2). Although there is some debate among scholars about the precise location of the area to which Paul is referring, it seems most likely to be the region near the south coast of Asia Minor, where he planted several churches on his first missionary journey; including the ones at Pisidian Antioch, Lystra, Derbe and Iconium, which we read about in Acts 13 – 14.

It is clear that, as Paul writes, a doctrinal controversy is seething among these young Galatian congregations, and Paul is deeply worried about it. Normally he begins his letters with complimentary remarks and prayerful good wishes. But all such conventions of tact and courtesy are swept aside in this letter. He has no interest in softening up his hearers with polite felicitations. After a perfunctory greeting, he launches into an impassioned and aggrieved rebuke.

> I am astonished that you are so quickly deserting the one who called you by the grace of Christ and are turning to a different gospel – which is really no gospel at all. Evidently some people are throwing you into confusion and are trying to pervert the gospel of Christ (1:6–7).

A group had arisen, then, holding a theological position contrary to that which Paul taught, and there was a real danger that the churches of Galatia would embrace their ideas. The situation was urgent. Some of the believers were already, as Paul writes, 'deserting'. And even those who hadn't yet done so were in a precarious state of bewilderment.

Paul leaves us in no doubt that he feels personally betrayed. A sense of injury sometimes colours his remarks, particularly in chapter 4 of his letter, as we shall see. But it would be unfair to dismiss Paul's strong language here in chapter 1 as simply due to pique. Rather, Paul's overwhelming concern is for the integrity of the gospel message. These theological rivals of his were undermining the Truth. And such a state of affairs simply could not be allowed. Paul was not prepared to tolerate it.

What was it that these rivals were teaching which could generate such indignation in the apostle? Paul doesn't tell us directly. We have to deduce it from what he says by way of reply. And that inevitably leaves room for a measure of uncertainty. It is a bit like listening to one end of a telephone conversation and trying to guess what the person is saying on the other end of the line. You can't be absolutely sure you have got it right. As a result, there has been a considerable amount of scholarly debate about the situation in Galatia.

Paul *versus* the Judaizers

One thing that is clear is that Paul's argument with this rival party in Galatia focused on the place of the Old Testament law. An important clue in this respect is near the end of the letter, where Paul says explicitly that they 'are trying to compel you to be circumcised' (6:12).

Christianity, of course, had been cradled in Judaism. Jesus himself, and all the early Christians, had been Jews. And to any Jew the law of Moses was of enormous significance. For over a thousand years that law had defined the nation of Israel as the people of God. It had enabled them to preserve their cultural identity in a pagan world in which many of them were forced to live as exiles. As a result, it was extraordinarily difficult for them to detach themselves, not just theologically, but emotionally, from their allegiance to that law.

Paul's missionary activity, however, was winning large numbers of non-Jews to Christianity. He was planting churches that had had no contact with the place where it had all begun, namely Jerusalem. These Galatian churches were a case in point. Most of the believers in Galatia were Gentiles. They knew little or nothing of the law of Moses. And Paul was notoriously outspoken in defending the view that there was no reason why they should. He taught that Gentile converts should be accepted into the full fellowship of the church on the basis of faith in Christ alone, without any additional legal conditions deriving from the Old Testament. But for some Jews this was simply too radical. It was inconceivable to them that Gentiles could be admitted into the covenant people of God with no requirement of submission to the law that for so long had been the hallmark of that people. So groups of conservative Jewish Christians emerged in the early church who sought to oppose Paul on this point. And it seems indisputable that these rival teachers who had invaded the Galatian churches were such a group.

In fact, it is very tempting to identify them with the Judaizing party that Luke tells us about in Acts 15. We learn there of a contingent of Jewish Christians from Jerusalem, some of them originally Pharisees, who insisted that Gentile Christians must be circumcised and required to obey the law of Moses. That scenario fits very well with precisely the kind of thing for which these stirrers in Galatia seem to be arguing.

This much, as I say, seems clear. Paul's rivals were Jews who felt that he did not give sufficient prominence to the law of Moses in his instruction to Gentile converts.

Legalists, racialists, nomists

It is when we try to specify the views of these Judaizers more precisely than that, however, that we begin to encounter scholarly disagreements. We do not have space to do justice to all the opinions that have been aired in this regard. If you are interested in knowing more about it,

Colin Kruse's book *Paul, the Law and Justification* (Apollos, 1995), ably reviews the scene. Suffice it to say that Paul probably takes issue, it seems to me, with three characteristics of these Judaizers.

First, they were *legalists*. A legalist is a person who believes that we must earn salvation by obeying God's rules. From Luke's description of them in Acts 15:1, it certainly does sound as if these Judaizers went that far. 'Unless you are circumcised, according to the custom taught by Moses, you cannot be saved,' they insisted.

Secondly, these Judaizers were *racialists*. They believed in the superiority of Jewish culture and wanted to maintain discriminatory practices that reflected that ethnic élitism. Some scholars have rightly pointed out that the laws these Judaizers were most concerned to impose on the Gentiles do not seem to have been the Ten Commandments. Indeed, it is very doubtful if any Christian in the early church (including Paul) disputed the continuing force of that moral law. Rather, the bits of the Old Testament law which these Judaizers made the most fuss about were those ceremonial regulations and sacramental rituals that acted as cultural markers for the Jewish people: things like dietary distinctives, Sabbath observance and, most of all, of course, circumcision. This suggests that the issue was one not only of moral merit but also of ethnic privilege. These Judaizers wanted to preserve the Jewishness of primitive Christianity by effectively insisting that every Gentile convert must become a Jewish proselyte too. They were, then, not just legalists but racialists too.

Thirdly, these Judaizers were *nomists*. Derived from *nomos*, the Greek word for 'law', this term has been coined by scholars to make a subtle but important distinction. Nomists are not necessarily legalists, because they may agree that obeying the law of God cannot earn us a place among God's covenant people. Nomists do, however, insist that such obedience is nevertheless a condition of retaining that privileged place within the covenant and enjoying its blessings. To use the language of traditional Christian theology, nomists believe that though the law cannot save us, it can and must sanctify us.

One of the anxieties that drove these Judaizers in Galatia to such a nomistic stance, I strongly suspect, was the fear that Gentile converts would bring pagan immorality into the church. As they saw it, Paul's gospel of free salvation was an open invitation to lax moral standards. If salvation is free, then we can sin with impunity! The remedy for such licentious logic, according to the nomist, is the law. The law enabled Old Testament Israel to preserve her moral distinctiveness during her exile in a pagan world, and it would enable the New Testament church to do the same.

In the course of studying this letter, we shall find Paul rebutting all three of these theological aberrations. Against the legalism that argues that salvation must be earned by obeying the law, Paul will insist that we are justified by faith, not works. That will be the theme of my second chapter, on Galatians 3:1–25. Against the racialism that wants to preserve Jewish privilege in the church, Paul will insist rather that among those baptized into the new-covenant community of the church, there can be no more barriers of race or culture, for all are one in Christ Jesus. That will be an important element in our third chapter, on Galatians 3:26 – 5:12. And against the nomism that argues that God's commandments are the key to living a holy life, Paul will insist instead that we are sanctified by the Spirit, not the law. That will be a major issue in our final chapter, looking at Galatians 5:13 – 6:18.

But before Paul can launch into such a systematic demolition of the errors of his rivals, he has to deal with an even more fundamental issue, namely his own apostolic authority. And that is the central issue, therefore, of the two opening chapters of his letter.

Undermining Paul

It is clear that the only way these Judaizers could hope to prosecute their theological agenda was by undermining Paul. It was he who had planted these churches in Galatia. It was he who had personally led many of these Gentile believers to Christ. If these Judaizers were going to have any success in their 'Back to Moses' campaign, it could only be by convincing these converts that Paul, their hero, had misled them. And it is evident from what Paul goes on to say in his letter that that was precisely the strategy they were adopting. Reading between the lines, it sounds as if they challenged Paul's authority on several grounds.

For a start, they argued that he was not one of the original twelve apostles, and that he taught an unorthodox version of Christianity as a result. 'Everything he teaches about Christianity that is right,' they said, 'he has learned from the apostles in Jerusalem. And everything he teaches that is wrong, he has made up himself!' (I am reminded of the would-be author whose work was returned by the publisher with the comment, 'Your work is both good and original. Unfortunately, the bit that is good isn't original, and the bit that is original isn't good!')

It sounds as if the Judaizers tried to drive a wedge between Paul and the apostle Peter in particular, making much of a rather unfortunate public altercation between

17

these two men that had occurred while Peter was in Antioch. And on top of this they seem to have cast doubt on the integrity of Paul's motives, suggesting that his liberal policy on circumcision was simply a concession designed to maximize the evangelistic response he obtained from Gentile audiences. 'He's just a cheap religious salesman looking for a popular line to hawk.'

Before Paul can begin to deal with the substance of their false teaching, therefore, he must first refute these libellous insinuations and re-establish his credentials among the Galatian believers. And this is what we find him doing in these first two chapters. We can summarize his response under two headings: he asserts that his is a message of divine origin, and a message of divine grace.

A message of divine origin
Certain of the truth?

It was Sunday morning, and Harry was lying on his bed browsing through a book he had bought the day before. Suddenly the telephone rang. It was Tom, Harry's neighbour from across the street.

'Hi, Harry! It's Tom. I just thought I . . .'

'Tom! How nice to hear from you! You don't usually ring this early. But I'm glad you have, because I want to tell you about this excellent book I've just got hold of. It really . . .'

'Harry! Will you please stop gibbering about books. I'm calling you about something very urgent. As I look out of my bedroom window I can see smoke coming from under your front door. Harry, I think your house is on fire!'

'Well, that is certainly a fascinating suggestion, Tom,

and I am really grateful to you for sharing your insight with me in this way. But as this book I've just been reading explains, can you be really sure of what you see, and can I be really sure of what you mean?'

'Eh?'

'Precisely, Tom! "Eh?" sums it up. As Professor Dubious says in his opening chapter, "with the decay of rationalism and logical positivism in late-twentieth-century western culture, question marks are all we have to share." It says on the flyleaf that he is one of our most celebrated postmodern philosophers, and I can quite see why. He puts it all so simply. The fact is, Tom, you and I can't be really certain about anything. You see smoke coming from my front door, and what do you do? Jump to the conclusion that my house is on fire! So rationalistic, Tom! So logical-positivist! So boringly left-brained! Where's your imagination? Anyone can see you haven't read any postmodern philosophy. If you had, you would realize that such a perception of things is totally subjective and relative. How do you know you're not dreaming? How do you know I haven't just burnt the toast? And how do I know I am correctly interpreting your words? Maybe you are just joking, or using a metaphor. Even if you had access to objective facts, Tom (which of course you don't), there is no way you can reliably communicate those facts to me. We are each locked in our own private world, you see, composing our own self-manufactured meta-narratives and thinking they are true. But everyone's truth is different, Tom. None of us has access to absolute truth. So nobody can tell us authoritatively what we ought to believe about anything. The best we can do is just to share our private question marks, as you have so generously done this morning, Tom. It's so kind of you to . . .'

'Harry! I don't know what kind of mystical gobbledygook

you picked up in that New Age bookshop yesterday afternoon. All I know is this. There is smoke coming from your front door, and while you have been rabbiting on, flames have started flickering behind your front-room curtains. Whether your postmodern philosopher would call this a meta-narrative on my part or not, I don't know. All I can say is, it certainly isn't a fairy-story, Harry! Granted that everyone is entitled to his or her own point of view, and that all perspectives are relative, I just feel that, as a friend, I ought to tell you that, in my humble and highly subjective opinion, your house is on fire! *If you stay there more than another ten seconds you are highly likely to fry! For goodness' sake, man, throw that useless book in the bin and get your bedroom window open. The fire-engine has just turned into the road. Can't you hear the siren? Or is that just a metaphor too? This isn't some Wittgensteinian language game we are playing, Harry. This is life or death!'*

Politically incorrect Paul

We live in a world which is reluctant to be certain about anything. I rather like that wall poster I saw in a student's room some months ago: 'The philosopher Descartes said the only thing he was certain about was his doubts. But how could he be so sure?'

These days, even agnosticism seems unacceptably doctrinaire. The scepticism of doubting Thomas has been displaced by the gullibility of Simple Simon. Rather than accept that if two people hold contradictory opinions, at least one of them must be wrong, we would rather deny the laws of logic and live with contradiction. Nobody is to be damned with that intolerant verdict, 'You're wrong.'

Everybody is to be affirmed. Everybody's opinion is to be accepted. Everybody is right!

And that, of course, is why Paul's outspokenness in this first chapter sounds so politically incorrect today, so uncongenial to our late-twentieth-century mindset.

To many of our contemporary theologians, the fact that some were preaching a different gospel in Galatia ought to have been no problem for Paul at all. According to their understanding of the nature of truth, we all have different gospels to some degree. The New Testament itself, they say, contains at least half a dozen different gospels within its own pages. There is Pauline theology and Petrine theology. There is the realized eschatology of the gospel of John, and the futurist eschatology of the Revelation of John. There is justification by faith in the book of Romans, and justification by works in the book of James. The list could go on and on. And once you open the Old Testament, of course, you discover even more diversity. Little wonder the church has been plagued by so much theological controversy down the years. Like those famous blind men who tried to describe an elephant, theologians have each taken one particular part of the Bible, interpreted it through the filter of their own spiritual experience, and then invested that personal theological insight with the status of absolute truth. 'The Bible says . . . !' they have arrogantly declared, when in point of fact what they should really have been saying is, 'This bit of the Bible means this to me.'

Haven't you heard people criticizing evangelical Christians today on these grounds? It seems so unfashionably unenlightened to take a dogmatic position on anything – unless, of course, your house is on fire!

Well, suffice it to say that Paul is not embarrassed by

dogma even if few of our contemporary theologians would be prepared to defend it. Unlike Harry's postmodernist Professor Dubious, Paul believed that there is such a thing as absolute truth, and he wasn't prepared to tolerate the contradiction of that truth. These rivals of his preached a 'different' gospel. And he would not have it! For, like Tom, he wasn't playing language games. An issue of life or death was at stake.

Anathema

We know from many other parts of his writings that Paul was prepared to be astonishingly eirenical and accommodating over a great many issues that threatened to cause division within the church. His letters are full of exhortations to 'maintain the unity of the Spirit'. But when this group of Judaizers arose in Galatia teaching a 'different gospel', we do not find Paul meekly accepting the situation as an expression of legitimate diversity within a theologically pluralistic church. On the contrary, he pronounces an awesome anathema upon those responsible. In 1:8–9, as we have seen, Paul calls down a curse on the head of anybody who distorts the gospel message, himself included, should he ever do so. 'Why,' he says, 'even if an angel from heaven turns up in your church one Sunday morning and, amid seraphic flame, teaches you something contrary to that message you heard from me at first, I say, let that angel be accursed too! That's how certain I am that the gospel I preached to you is true. Be assured that this is no mere hysterical outburst on my part, born of my wounded feelings. Let me repeat it to prove my earnestness in this matter. These Judaizers in your midst are not just liars, they are damned liars. The message they propagate will not just lead you astray, it will lead you to hell!'

Am I now trying to win the approval of men, or of God? Or am I trying to please men? (1:10).

In other words, Paul is saying: 'Does that sound like the language of a man-pleaser to you? Am I just shaping my words to make a favourable impression on you, as they make out I do? You know perfectly well I am not a man-pleaser and never have been. There may have been a time in my life when I worried about what other people thought of me, but not any longer. No, I am a servant of Jesus Christ now, and ever since I received his commission it has been my sole business in life to declare the message he gave me without fear or favour, without distortion or compromise. Make no mistake about it, Galatians, this gospel message I preach is Truth, Truth with a capital T. And you cannot negotiate about such truth.'

Special message, special messenger

I want you to know, brothers, that the gospel I preached is not something that man made up. I did not receive it from any man, nor was I taught it; rather, I received it by revelation from Jesus Christ (1:11–12).

If this gospel message Paul is talking about had been merely the product of Paul's own theological reflection, then of course the strong language of his anathema would have been arrogant and misplaced. But Paul tells us here that the content of this message he preached had been given to him in a direct, unmediated fashion by Jesus

Christ himself. It was not therefore a human suggestion, opinion, hypothesis or speculation. To use Paul's own word, it was 'revelation'. It did not originate in his or any other human mind. It came from the mind of God.

And that didn't just make the gospel special. It made Paul special too. It meant he possessed a title which none of those Judaizers in Galatia could claim. He announces it in the very first line of the letter:

> Paul, an apostle – sent not from men nor by man, but by Jesus Christ and God the Father, who raised him from the dead (1:1).

The apostles were first-generation Christians. They did not rely for their understanding of the gospel on traditions passed down to them by others. Rather, they possessed a unique, first-hand, God-given mandate to define the gospel for others.

In the section that begins in 1:16 and goes on to 2:10, it is noticeable how keen Paul is to draw the attention of the Galatians to his own theological independence in this regard. Nobody had taught him the Christian message. Even if the early church in Jerusalem had wanted to do so, it had no opportunity to instruct him in the rudiments of the Christian gospel, for he spent the first three years after his conversion in Arabia and Damascus. Even when he did go to Jerusalem for the first time, it was only a brief, private visit to meet Peter and James. As far as the church in Jerusalem as a whole was concerned, Paul remained a total stranger for the first fourteen years of his Christian life. There was no way he could have learnt his understanding of the gospel from them. His claim is that this was given to him direct by Christ.

But the Judaizers in the Galatian church were taking that original apostolic gospel which he had received and were 'perverting it' – that is, literally, turning it back to front. Such a sacrilegious distortion of the truth Paul could not allow. As Elijah the prophet of old had thundered against idolatry, so Paul the apostle thunders against these false teachers. How can he be sure he is right and they are wrong, you ask? For the same reason that that Old Testament prophet could. He had experienced divine revelation. He knew that the message for which he stood was inspired. And that knowledge freed him from self-doubt and endowed him with a remarkable authority among the people of God.

It was that authority that the Judaizers were seeking to undermine. And it was that authority, therefore, that Paul had to defend, not for the sake of his own pride, but for the sake of the gospel: the gospel of which he was a God-appointed custodian. It was truth! And you cannot negotiate about truth.

A message of divine grace

Through the law I died to the law so that I might live for God. I have been crucified with Christ and I no longer live, but Christ lives in me. The life I live in the body, I live by faith in the Son of God, who loved me and gave himself for me. I do not set aside the grace of God, for if righteousness could be gained through the law, then Christ died for nothing! (2:19–21).

These verses are in many respects a summary of the argument which Paul is going to develop throughout the rest of this letter. The key word in them is 'grace', which occurs twice earlier in these first two chapters: both the believers (1:6) and Paul (1:15) were called by God's grace.

The meaning of grace

What that word 'grace' means to you I don't know. My fear is that to many in our day it is almost unintelligible. About twenty years ago, a group of Christian students conducted a survey by questionnaire in preparation for an evangelistic mission. One question tested people's familiarity with the word 'grace'. They had to put a tick beside the word that corresponded closest in their understanding to its meaning; about ten choices were offered. The fascinating result was that about 90% of people put their tick beside words like 'charm', 'elegance', 'beauty' or 'style'. A small number opted for meanings like 'thanksgiving', 'prayer' or 'benediction' (influenced, I guess, by the idea of grace before meals). But only a tiny handful expressed any awareness at all of that definition clearly listed in the Oxford dictionary, namely 'gift', 'favour' or 'kindness'.

Quite frankly I was appalled. It made me appreciate the danger of jargon, even biblical jargon! Preachers like me had better realize that these days, when we say that Jesus Christ is full of grace, most of our listeners will probably imagine the Saviour to be a ballet dancer or a male model!

Of course, that's not what Paul means by the word here. 'Grace' for Paul is not the opposite of clumsiness, but the opposite of merit. Grace is favour extended to undeserving people as a gift. And as a result of the unusual circumstances of his conversion, no member of the early church had a greater sensitivity to and appreciation of the word.

In the section from 1:11 onwards, Paul is sketching some of the history of his apostolic calling. He reminds the Galatians of the man he used to be: a fanatical Jewish fundamentalist who went far beyond these Judaizing rivals of his in his enthusiasm for the religion of Moses. 'Why,' he says in verses 13–14, 'I was a rising star in the rabbinical schools of Jerusalem, surpassing my peers both in my academic prowess and in my religious commitment. Indeed, so passionate was I where Judaism was concerned that I even sought to persecute the Christians. Implacable in my hatred of them, I was obsessed with the idea not just of punishing them but of exterminating them. I wanted to destroy the church.'

But then, suddenly, it all changed. Like a magnet that has its polarity reversed, so Paul's life suddenly swung round to point in totally the opposite direction.

'God . . . was pleased to reveal his Son in me,' he says (1:15–16).

Notice very particularly the way Paul speaks of this dramatic change in his life. In verses 13–14 the subject of the verbs is always 'I'. 'I persecuted the church.' 'I was advancing in Judaism.' But in verses 15–16 God suddenly seizes the centre of the stage, and Paul becomes the object rather than the subject of the verbs in three places.

First, he says, 'God . . . set me apart from birth.' That's where it began. Not on the Damascus road but in his mother's womb. Paul realized now that God had a plan for his life before he had a life to plan.

From that pre-natal election, he goes on, secondly, to speak of the divine summons he subsequently received.

And God was the subject of that action too. 'God called me by his grace.' Paul perhaps thinks of God as an oriental potentate extending a generous invitation to some insignificant and unworthy peasant in his vast empire. 'Come, Paul. I want you in my royal service!'

But God is not content merely to issue this invitation from a distance. He adds to Paul's external call an internal call also. So, thirdly, 'God . . . was pleased to reveal his Son in me.' Notice that preposition 'in'. It is a little unexpected. We expect Paul to say 'to me'. But Paul is thinking here not only of that miracle by which the risen Christ was presented to his physical eyes on the Damascus road, but also of the miraculous way in which his inward, spiritual eyes were opened to understand who that glorious person was and to embrace him by faith.

'God set me apart . . . called me . . . revealed his Son in me.' Here is the root of Paul's gospel of grace. It lies in his own experience of the gift.

And it was only at the point at which God had completed his work of grace in Paul that some measure of initiative was returned to Paul's own hands once again: '. . . that I might preach him among the Gentiles'. From a conversion in which Paul is passive issues a commission in which he is to be decidedly active. Paul's experience of grace sends him out into the world with a message of grace.

Paul, grace and law

We might have thought that the anti-Christian fanaticism of Paul's earlier life rendered any office in the church out of the question. Least of all would we have considered him an ideal candidate for missionary work. Paul had been a *legalist*, establishing his own self-righteousness by the merits of his religious zeal. He had been a *nomist*, combating the sinful lusts of his flesh by the iron discipline of God's law. And most of all he had been a *racialist*, convinced that his circumcision had granted him membership of the most spiritually privileged and superior people on earth. He was a Jew – a Jew by birth, a Jew by conviction, a Jew by practice. As far as he was concerned, the Gentiles were to be at best pitied and at worst despised. Didn't the rabbis say that the Gentiles had been created by God only to fuel the flames of hell? What could God be thinking about, making a man like Paul his apostle to the Gentiles?

God's wisdom in this matter was wiser than human wisdom, as is so often the case. For the fact is that God's extraordinarily gracious initiative in Paul's life not only turned his opinion of Jesus Christ upside down, it revolutionized his attitude towards the law of Moses and towards the Gentiles too.

Paul knew himself to be a trophy of God's grace. He hadn't deserved the generosity God had showered upon him. Quite the opposite! To think of it! He had tried to destroy the church! 'Saul, Saul, why do you persecute me?' Those words of the glorified Christ on the Damascus road remained burnt into Paul's heart for the rest of his life. He never got over the amazement of it all. That God should have mercy on someone like him, the chief of sinners! 'I am not fit to be called an apostle,' he would confess to the Corinthians, 'for I persecuted the church. Nevertheless, by the grace of God I am what I am!' (*cf.* 1 Cor. 15:9–10).

As Paul's Spirit-inspired mind got to work on this truth that Christ had revealed to him, this grace that he had

29

shown to him, the revolution in Paul's theological perspective began to take place. What God had done through Christ on the cross meant that, in his grace, he could forgive the appalling crimes Paul had committed and commission him to be an apostle.

What had become of Paul's legalistic quest for an acceptance before God based on his own merits? It was exposed as an arrogant exercise in human pride. We only add to our sin when, in our impertinence, we try to achieve such a boastful, self-manufactured salvation. That 'I' which had dominated Paul's early life is crucified with Christ.

What had become of Paul's nomistic quest for moral perfection by obedience to God's law? It too was exposed as futile. We fallen creatures simply are not capable of such perfect obedience. The attempt to attain it renders Judaism, even at its highest and best, a religious dead-end that can lead only to a depressing sense of failure and condemnation. Through the law we die.

Most of all, what has become of Paul's racialistic sense of Jewish cultural superiority? It has been demolished. Pious Jews like him need the grace of God as much, or even more than, any Gentile. In fact, as we shall see in our next chapter, once the spiritual blinkers were off Paul's eyes he quickly began to realize that God's whole purpose according to the Old Testament Scriptures was to save the Gentiles. Paul's former contempt for the Gentiles had been utterly misplaced. In this period of the last days which the coming of Jesus, the Messiah, had inaugurated, God planned to bring great numbers of Gentiles into his kingdom. And Paul had been called to reap that spiritual harvest.

All this was an extraordinarily liberating discovery for Paul. He who had been bound hand and foot by the guilt-inducing restrictions of his Judaistic background suddenly found himself free! He was free from the fear of final judgment, from the shame of moral failure, and from the arrogance of racial pride.

He could mix with Christians of any race now, in the conviction that whatever their pagan past, they had been called by the free grace of God just as he had been. It was no longer a matter of whether a rabbi had circumcised you. It was a matter of whether God had revealed his Son in you or not.

The more Paul reflected on this matter, the more dramatic did the sociological implications of the gospel seem. As he would later write in his letter to the Ephesians, God had broken down the wall of partition that separated Jew from Gentile, and had constructed a new race out of the two – the Christian race – united not by genetic solidarity but by the shared experience of the Spirit of Christ within.

And the more Paul thought about that, the more he realized that the whole nature of the gospel as a message of divine grace was at stake in this issue of Gentile converts and the Jewish law. That's why we find him taking such a strong line on the issue here in his letter to the Galatians. To force Gentiles to observe the Jewish law was a fundamental denial of the centrality of grace. As he puts it in 2:21, it was to 'set aside the grace of God'. Paul tells us emphatically that he will not do that!

Two matters of principle

He goes on in chapter 2 to recount two incidents which were of special significance in this respect. Here is his account of the first.

Paul meets the Jerusalem leaders

Fourteen years later I went up again to Jerusalem, this time with Barnabas. I took Titus along also. I went in response to a revelation and set before them the gospel that I preach among the Gentiles. But I did this privately to those who seemed to be leaders, for fear that I was running or had run my race in vain. Yet not even Titus, who was with me, was compelled to be circumcised, even though he was a Greek. This matter arose because some false brothers had infiltrated our ranks to spy on the freedom we have in Christ Jesus and to make us slaves. We did not give in to them for a moment, so that the truth of the gospel might remain with you.

As for those who seemed to be important – whatever they were makes no difference to me; God does not judge by external appearance – those men added nothing to my message. On the contrary, they saw that I had been entrusted with the task of preaching the gospel to the Gentiles, just as Peter had been to the Jews. For God, who was at work in the ministry of Peter as an apostle to the Jews, was also at work in my ministry as an apostle to the Gentiles. James, Peter and John, those reputed to be pillars, gave me and Barnabas the right hand of fellowship when they recognised the grace given to me. They agreed that we should go to the Gentiles, and they to the Jews. All they asked was that we should continue to remember the poor, the very thing I was eager to do (2:1–10).

This was obviously a traumatic incident. Paul's grammar seems to deteriorate a bit with the emotional stress of recalling it. It sounds as though these 'false brothers' mentioned in verse 4 belonged to precisely the same group of Judaizers that was causing trouble in Galatia. They were challenging the orthodoxy of Paul's gospel even then, and demanding, it seems (among other things) that Titus, one of Paul's Gentile converts accompanying his party, should be circumcised.

Notice the reason Paul gives for the defiance of his response to them: 'We did not give in to them for a moment, so that the truth of the gospel might remain with you' (verse 5).

The issue was that of truth. By insisting that Gentile converts should be circumcised and bound by the Jewish law, these Judaizers were perpetuating a religious system that Christ had made redundant. They were undermining 'the truth of the gospel'. Fortunately, the other apostles in Jerusalem were clear enough on this point to realize that Paul was right, and the result of their high-level consultation was therefore unambiguous. Titus was not compelled to be circumcised. No change or addition to the message Paul preached was required or even suggested. On the contrary, the apostles endorsed his missionary calling to the Gentiles and publicly identified with it by offering him and his colleague Barnabas the right hand of fellowship.

Paul challenges Peter

Sadly, however, old habits die hard, as Paul learnt as a result of the second incident he goes on to recall.

> When Peter came to Antioch, I opposed him to his face, because he was clearly in the wrong. Before certain men came from James, he used to eat with the Gentiles. But when they arrived, he began to draw back and separate himself from the Gentiles because he was afraid of those who belong to the circumcision group. The other Jews joined him in his hypocrisy, so that by their hypocrisy even Barnabas was led astray (2:11–13).

Can you imagine how this incident must have devastated Paul? It was bad enough that these emissaries from James should still be locked in their old racist prejudices about not eating with Gentiles, but that Peter should so weakly follow their lead, closely followed by the other Jewish Christians present, including even Paul's closest colleague Barnabas – why, the apostle must have felt betrayed by just about everyone. A lesser man would undoubtedly have given in, but not Paul. This was a crucial matter of principle for him, and he was determined not to duck it. Notice again the explanation he gives for his uncompromising response to the situation.

> When I saw that they were not acting in line with the truth of the gospel, I said to Peter in front of them all, 'You are a Jew, yet you live like a Gentile and not like a Jew. How is it, then, that you force Gentiles to follow Jewish customs?' (2:14).

What a moment! Can you imagine the silence that fell in the room as the apostles Paul and Peter faced one another in this tense stand-off?

Paul felt he had to risk the embarrassment and scandal of the confrontation because, as he tells us in verses 11–16, Peter was clearly in the wrong on two counts.

First, *his behaviour was inconsistent*. 'Come on, Peter. You know perfectly well that you enjoy a pork chop with the rest of us these days! So how come you have suddenly rediscovered all your old Jewish scruples and are insisting that our Gentile brothers in Christ must be circumcised before you can eat in their company? You're just playing a part, Peter, for the sake of these conservative Jews from Jerusalem whom you want to impress. It's all a shameful charade. It's hypocrisy!'

Secondly, *his theology was inconsistent*. If Peter's actions had been motivated by sensitivity to the conscience of some inadequately taught visitors to the church, Paul would probably have been happy to overlook the matter. As he argues in Romans 14, the strong Christian should always be prepared, in love, to concede to the scruples of weaker brothers and sisters. But that was not Peter's motivation. Peter was being theologically intimidated and confused by this circumcision party, and was putting the truth of the gospel in jeopardy as a result.

Paul's reasoning then continues with the magnificent words already quoted, about being crucified with Christ, living by faith in the Son of God, and not setting aside God's grace by attempting to gain righteousness through the law (2:19–21). In many respects, as I said earlier, these verses represent a highly compressed summary of all that Paul is going to argue in much greater detail in the rest of this letter. So I don't intend to unpack this summary thoroughly now. Suffice it to say that in these few sentences Paul is outlining to Peter (and to anyone else) why it is that the legalism, the nomism and the racialism of these Judaizers are totally inconsistent with the Christian gospel.

As far as the legalism is concerned, he is sure that Peter is already with him.

'Christian Jews like you and me, Peter, have learnt the folly of trying to earn our own salvation by good works. We have trusted Christ as our Saviour precisely because we know we cannot be saved any other way. We have been justified (that is, declared righteous in God's sight) by faith and not by observing the law. Whatever flirtations with legalism we engaged in during our old days in Judaism, they have been abandoned since we became Christians. You cannot be a Christian and a legalist, Peter. We both recognize that.

'Why then are these Judaizers still pushing the Jewish law on to the Gentiles, brother?

'They will tell us, Peter, that they are not legalists, but nomists. Their concern, they will say, is not with how people become Christians, but with what kind of moral lifestyle they display as Christians. They will tell us that if we don't make the Gentiles obey the law it will be the thin end of the wedge. No circumcision today, no sexual chastity tomorrow.

'For the sake of argument, let's suppose that they are right. What if people like us, Peter – people who profess to be saved by Christ – prove to be less than perfect in our subsequent moral behaviour? Does that mean there is some fundamental defect in the gospel? Does it mean that Christ promotes sin (2:17)? Does the gospel save us from the sin of the past only to throw us back on to the same old treadmill of law in order to remedy the sin of the present? I say, absolutely not! The answer to sin in a believer's life, Peter, is not the law. To say that it is, as the nomists do, is to reconstruct Judaism under the veneer of Christianity. It is to "rebuild what I destroyed" (2:18). No, the answer to sin in the life of a believer is Christ – Christ crucified, Christ risen, Christ alive inside the Christian.'

Paul is arguing to Peter that although nomism may be slightly more theologically respectable than its first cousin legalism, in practice it has the same consequences. Whether you try to earn your salvation by observing the law (as the legalist does), or to demonstrate your salvation by observing the law (as the nomist does), both strategies have the effect of devaluing the work of Christ.

'I refuse to undermine the centrality of grace!' insists Paul. 'I do not set aside the grace of God' (2:21). For if righteousness could be gained, either as a legal status or as a moral state, through the law, then the work of Christ is an irrelevancy. He died for nothing! And that isn't just hypocrisy, that is downright heresy.

'Peter, don't you realize, when you turn your back on those Gentile brothers of ours simply because they aren't circumcised, that that is what you are in effect saying? You are saying that Christ died for nothing!'

This is why our study of this letter to the Galatians is so important.

Truth today

Maybe all this talk about Judaizers and the law, legalism and nomism, sounds rather technical and remote from practical issues of Christian living. Maybe you are thinking to yourself, 'These Bible studies are too much like a

37

theology lecture for me. I'll try something else that doesn't stretch my brain quite so much!'

I can sympathize with you. I have had quite a struggle getting my head round this letter too. But stay with me as we try to work out what this profound Christian thinker, Paul, is saying. For I promise you that it is extraordinarily relevant and important to you and to me.

Paul is telling us that there is such a thing as truth and that it is not negotiable. We need to hear that statement today, for we live in an age when the very idea of truth is under attack. We can learn from Paul the importance of making a stand on this vital issue.

First, great Christians can let the side down sometimes where the truth is concerned. Peter was, like Paul, an apostle. But on this occasion in Antioch he made a mistake. If Peter erred in that way, how much more will lesser Christian heroes sometimes do the same! This is why we should never lend our support uncritically to any Christian leader, no matter how eminent his or her reputation. Every one of us is responsible before God to understand for ourselves controversial theological issues to the best of our ability.

Secondly, pressure groups in the church have power to obscure the truth. Peter would not have made his mistake if he had not been looking over his shoulder at that influential party of Jews from Jerusalem. Isn't it so often the way? We act, not out of personal conscience, but out of a conformist desire for acceptance and approval by others. It takes a great deal of courage to stand up in public, as Paul did, and refuse to be intimidated. But there are times when we must find that courage, or live with the shame of hypocrisy.

Thirdly, it is supremely important to make a public stand for the truth when necessary. Of course, there are people who think they are doing this when in fact they are just being downright obstructive and pompous. Lord Moran complained of Charles de Gaulle once: 'The man is stuffed so full of principles, there is no room left for even a little Christian tolerance!'

On the whole, we much prefer to deal with people who are prepared to be flexible about things, and willing to negotiate.

'Don't rock the boat!' we say.

'Anything for a quiet life!'

'Least said, soonest mended!'

This is the creed of twentieth-century pragmatism. As Stanley Baldwin put it: 'I would rather be an opportunist and float than go to the bottom with my principles round my neck.' This is why our age has produced many politicians but very few martyrs. It seems to us recklessly extremist to fight for a cause, let alone to die for it. How did that classic proverb put it? 'Better red than dead!'

Let Paul teach us that, despite our contemporary preference for pragmatists, there are occasions when a man or woman of principle is neither a bigot nor a trouble-maker, but a hero.

Conscience must never be sacrificed on the altar of expediency. There are times when, like Martin Luther, we have to dig in our heels and say, 'Here I stand, I can do no other. So help me God!' Let us learn from Paul's example to be militant in defence of the truth of the Christian gospel.

Truth and tolerance

Some time ago I received two letters which caused me deep sadness. They both came from former Cambridge students who used to attend my church, and had been keen members of the university Christian Union. They wrote to tell me why they felt unable any longer to call themselves evangelical Christians. Although they had come to this conclusion by different routes, the ultimate reason behind their abdication of faith was the same in each case. They both found evangelical Christianity 'too self-assured', 'too reluctant to accommodate other people's ideas', 'too narrow-minded' and 'too dogmatic'. In short, evangelical Christianity was too unfashionably certain about truth in this hyper-tolerant, pluralistic, postmodernist world of ours. Like Harry, they had read Professor Dubious, and felt that their old Christian Union friends were exaggerating the seriousness of the smoke coming from under the front door. They wanted to keep a more open mind on the issue.

Please do not misunderstand me on this point. I am, I think, by temperament an open-minded and non-judgmental person. I can sympathize considerably with the disillusionment both these students had experienced at the hands of what I suspect was an excessively defensive and rigidly doctrinaire evangelicalism in the churches they had attended on leaving Cambridge. I confess I have often found myself embarrassed and exasperated by the bigotry and obscurantism of some of my evangelical colleagues in ministry who use the phrase 'The Bible says . . .' in an irresponsible way to support an unwarranted authoritarianism in matters that ought to be left to the conscience of the individual believer. Far more claims to infallibility have been issued from the pulpits of evangelical churches, I fear, than have ever come out of the Vatican!

I can understand how university students who have been trained academically to respect diversity of opinion and to live with it might find the preaching of some evangelicals intolerant and arrogant. But – and it is a very big 'but' –

there are some things that remain non-negotiable in the Christian faith. Paul tells us in this letter that the Christian gospel is an inspired message, a message of Truth with a capital T.

We must not yield to that infantile definition of faith as 'believing what you know ain't true'. This is nonsense! Faith for the Christian is not a convenient psychological prop. We believe under the constraint of the truth. The truth of the gospel demands faith, as smoke under a door demands action.

In this respect there has to be a limit to one's tolerance. For tolerance without limits isn't real tolerance at all, but simply indifference. It is to confuse an open mind with an empty mind! Well did G. K. Chesterton observe: 'The object of opening the mind, as of opening the mouth, is to shut it again on something solid.' It is one thing humbly to submit our Christian convictions to critical scrutiny. It is another thing altogether to behave as if we have no convictions at all.

Paul is telling us in these first two chapters of Galatians that a verbal message lies at the foundation of Christianity. He calls it the 'gospel'. And that message is true.

To allow people to distort that message or to mispresent it is not laudable tolerance, but crass irresponsibility. No matter how much we detest religious bigotry, we mustn't allow either sentimentality or spinelessness to soften us on that point. The gospel is simply not open to negotiation. If we behave as if it is, two things will happen in consequence.

First, the world will come to the conclusion that our message is one they can ignore with impunity, just as Harry was tempted to ignore Tom's phone call.

Secondly, a door of opportunity will be left open to less

41

weak-kneed belief systems. False religions which have the courage of their convictions, erroneous though those convictions are, will fill the spiritual vacuum. Our world, in all its postmodern doubts, is hungry for some sense of meaning to existence. But it will never be convinced that Christ can satisfy that hunger if we go soft on truth. Many will be seduced by the claims of various fundamentalist sects instead.

Whatever you do, do not accept any compromise on this issue. If you do, Paul's anathema of 1:8–9 will fall upon you too. You cannot negotiate, you see, about truth.

2

An irrevocable promise
Galatians 3:1–25

When I was an undergraduate, I had the good fortune to be resident in a hall where the Scottish theologian William Neil was warden. The thing I remember about him was the way, from his diminutive stature of no more than 5ft 4ins, he was able to cast terror into the entire student body.

A good example was provided by the address he always delivered to freshers following the first formal dinner of term. After a few pleasant stories from the past to lull us into a false sense of security, he would turn his attention to the hall rules. These ran to four sides of A4, and we were all given a copy almost as soon as we set foot in the building. Dr Neil would indicate this formidable sheaf of regulations with a bland smile. 'I believe', he would say, beaming and almost with a wink, 'that rules are for the guidance of wise men.'

He paused, and there was an almost audible sigh of relief as anxious new students thanked their lucky stars that they had been placed in the charge of one who was clearly enlightened and liberal-minded.

Then, as Neil saw the cheered countenances about him, his expression would change from a benign smile to a belligerent scowl, such as one normally associates with regimental sergeant-majors in the drill hall. As our faces dissolved into consternation, he would add: 'Aye, for the guidance of wise men and the obedience of fools!' We were not left in much doubt about which of those two categories all first-year undergraduates belonged to.

The theology of rules

Paul is much concerned in his letter with rules. For, as you will remember from chapter 1, a group of Judaistic false teachers had infiltrated the churches of Galatia, arguing that rules were immensely important. They were intended not just for general guidance but for pedantic obedience.

'You can't have a relationship with God just as you are,' the teachers were telling the young Christians there. 'You must do something to be worthy of it. You must be circumcised, and observe all the rules and regulations which Moses laid down in the Old Testament. You must not presume to be one of his covenant people unless you meet these requirements of his covenant law.'

As we indicated in that chapter, this theology of rules operated on three levels with the false teachers. First, they were legalists, who said you must earn the right to have a relationship with God through obedience to the law. Secondly, they were racialists, who said that a relationship with God was a Jewish privilege, and therefore restricted to those who were circumcised and kept the law as Jews did.

Thirdly, they were nomists, who said that obedience to the law was the way to maintain a relationship with God once you had got it.

Legalism *versus* faith

Paul is seeking to rebut all three of these aspects of their error. And in chapter 3 of his letter, which is the focus of this chapter, he begins by tackling the issue of legalism. He musters four arguments, all with the same underlying goal of convincing the Galatian Christians that the key to a relationship with God is not rules at all, but faith.

An argument from the experience of the early church

> I would like to learn just one thing from you: Did you receive the Spirit by observing the law, or by believing what you heard? Are you so foolish? After beginning with the Spirit, are you now trying to attain your goal by human effort? (3:2–3).

'Christianity', points out Paul, 'didn't begin with some philosopher propounding a new moral rule. It began when a group of believers received a new moral energy. The promise of Jesus was: "You will receive power when the Holy Spirit comes on you" (Acts 1:8). On the day of Pentecost, that is exactly what happened.'

Paul's reasoning with the churches of Galatia runs on like this. 'You Galatians know this at first hand. For when as an apostle of Jesus Christ I brought the gospel to you, those pentecostal signs accompanied it. Indeed, the Spirit is still miraculously active among you even now in my absence.

'Answer me this simple question. Is this mighty revolutionary Spirit associated in your experience with keeping religious rules? You know he isn't! The Jews had been keeping their religious rules for a thousand years and nothing like this ever happened to them. The Holy Spirit wasn't a prize you won for your good works. He is a gift you received when you believed the gospel message.

'Well then, you daft bunch! How can you be so dumb as to think that the God who has blessed you so remarkably in the past, without any contribution in the way of observing religious rules on your part, is going to bless you more in future if you start offering him such religiosity now?'

> Have you suffered so much for nothing – if it really was for nothing? Does God give you his Spirit and work miracles among you because you observe the law, or because you believed what you heard? (3:4–5).

That word 'suffered' may imply that the Galatians had endured persecution for the sake of the gospel. We know from the book of Acts that the local Jewish community gave Paul and his friends a very hard time when he first evangelized their region. In fact, Paul got perilously close to being stoned to death there at one point. So it is more than possible that after his departure the small congregation of new believers he left behind continued to suffer harassment. If they did, it is clear that as far as Paul is concerned, such suffering was rendered pointless if they had now come to the conclusion that the Jews who were causing them the suffering were right all the time.

'If you really think', continues Paul, 'that there is more

to be gained by a life of bondage to the Jewish law than by a life of freedom in the Spirit, why then, you have learnt nothing from your early Christian experience – nothing at all!'

An argument from the example of Abraham

Consider Abraham: 'He believed God, and it was credited to him as righteousness' (3:6).

This is a shrewd tactical move on Paul's part, of course, for none of his Judaistic opponents could fault the theological *bona fides* of Abraham. As far as circumcision was concerned, he was the one who had started the whole show. With the possible exception of Moses, there was no figure of Jewish history they were likely to regard with higher favour.

'Yet', reasons Paul, 'what does the Bible actually say about Abraham's relationship with God? Was it based on the performance of religious works like circumcision? Not at all! The book of Genesis says: "He believed God, and it was credited to him as righteousness."'

Now, we have to be a bit careful about this verse. It uses a Hebrew idiom which is easy to misunderstand in English translation. 'Credited to him as righteousness' sounds as if God accepted Abraham's faith as a substitute for moral obedience. His belief was 'credited to him' in the place of, or as a form of, 'righteousness'. But that isn't what Paul means. In a parallel passage in Romans 4, he makes it abundantly clear that faith must not be thought of as some kind of alternative good work, the merit of which makes us acceptable to God. The Hebrew idiom 'credited as righteousness' in fact means the very opposite of that. When someone does not do any good works, but simply trusts God to justify him in spite of his wickedness, that person's faith is credited to him as righteousness (see Romans 4:5).

In other words, Abraham's special relationship with God wasn't earned by his faith. It was an act of divine generosity, rather like someone giving you a birthday present by transferring money into your bank account. All Abraham's faith did was to accept the gift. He certainly wasn't saved by circumcision, because, as Paul argues in that same passage of Romans, he didn't even receive that sign until years later. Rather, he was saved because he believed. And that principle of justification by faith didn't end with him!

> Understand, then, that those who believe are children of Abraham. The Scripture foresaw that God would justify the Gentiles by faith, and announced the gospel in advance to Abraham: 'All nations will be blessed through you.' So those who have faith are blessed along with Abraham, the man of faith (3:7–9).

Ironically, far from being an ally to these legalistic Judaizers, then, Abraham actually turns out to be the archetypal believer. The promise God gave him was a gospel promise. It had nothing to do with the Jewish law at all. God declared to this man, two millennia before it happened, his intention of bringing people from every nation on the face of the earth into an experience of blessing through Abraham. Abraham had believed that covenant vow. Paul is saying that the Galatians are the living proof of its fulfilment. Properly understood, those Judaizers who were confusing them weren't the true children of Abraham at all – the Galatians were! For the true children of Abraham are descended from him not physically but spiritually. They share not his genes but his faith.

An argument from the inevitability of human moral failure

> All who rely on observing the law are under a curse, for it is written: 'Cursed is everyone who does not continue to do everything written in the Book of the Law' (3:10).

If referring to Abraham was tactically ingenious, then Paul's argument here must rank as a master-stroke, for he is quoting from the book of Leviticus, a book crammed with the very laws which these Judaizers were so keen to make the Gentile Christians observe.

'Look,' Paul says, 'you only have to read the Old Testament law more closely to discover that it tells you itself that it can't save anybody. And that is for a very simple reason: nobody can possibly keep it.'

As far as God is concerned, keeping the law isn't like sitting an exam, where you get a pass provided you score 51% (or even less!). God's standards of righteousness demand 100% obedience, 100% of the time. It is like carrying a sheet of fragile glass – one slip and it is shattered. As James puts it in his letter: 'Whoever keeps the whole law and yet stumbles at just one point is guilty of breaking all of it' (James 2:10).

True, there is potentially a blessing in the law. But it is a blessing which is utterly inaccessible and unattainable, for the law says: 'The man who does these things will live by them' (3:12). There is no-one on the face of the globe who has ever fulfilled that condition of total obedience to God's satisfaction. So instead of inheriting that tantalizing blessing of life which Leviticus talks about, all the law does is to render us human beings ever more inescapably the object of God's judgment. 'Cursed is everyone who does not continue to do everything written in the Book of the Law' (3:10). That's what the law itself says. And 'cursed', therefore, is what anybody who relies on religious rules for salvation is bound to end up being.

'If you are still in any doubt about my biblical warrant for coming to that pessimistic conclusion,' argues Paul, 'then just think about the message of the Old Testament prophets. Take Habakkuk, for instance. He lived through a period of appalling divine judgment, when that "curse" that lies upon those who break God's covenant law was clearly expressed in the political and economic disasters which befell the people of Israel. Habakkuk knew the law of God inside out. But was it the possibility of keeping that law better that gave him hope for the future? No, read Habakkuk carefully and you will find that he anticipated an age to come when the life and the righteousness that the law was inadequate to provide would be freely bestowed on God's people, not because they kept religious rules at all, but because they put their trust in God.'

An argument from the purpose of the law

Clearly no-one is justified before God because of the law, because, 'The righteous will live by faith' (3:11).

With that, Paul embarks on the fourth and final argument of the chapter. To be frank, it is a notoriously difficult section to follow. Paul's logic is extremely compressed, or even muddled. Unsympathetic critics have sometimes suggested that his logic is completely non-existent! One commentator claims there are over 300 different interpretations of verse 20 alone! I don't want you therefore to feel discouraged if this next section proves heavy going at times. Basically what Paul is arguing is that even within its own terms of reference, the Old Testament law was never intended to save anybody anyway.

Here is a short tale to help illustrate this point.

Once upon a time, in a land far away, there were two childhood sweethearts. The girl was the daughter of a wealthy count; the boy a humble shoemaker's son. They swore a secret vow to one another that when they came of age they would marry, and as a token of the pledge they exchanged rings.

All through their childhood years they rejoiced in the hope of that wedding day to come. But as they grew older a hesitation began to enter the young man's heart. His desire to marry the girl was as strong as ever, but adult understanding had brought with it an adult awareness of the difference between their social backgrounds.

'I can't marry you as I am, just a cobbler's son!' he told her.

'Of course you can!' she replied. 'Your lack of nobility makes no difference to me.'

But the boy could not believe her.

'No,' he said. 'Before we can be married I must do something to prove I am worthy of you.' So he left her weeping, to seek his fortune in the wide world.

He thought at first he would try the army. 'If I can win many decorations in battle, then I will be worthy of her love,' he said to himself. But unfortunately the young man was no hero. He fled from the battlefield in cowardice, was stripped of such minor rank as he had achieved, and was discharged from the army in disgrace.

'Perhaps I could become rich and prosperous instead,' he reasoned. 'Then I would be worthy of her love.' So he entered commerce with the little capital he had saved. But, alas, the young man had no head for business either. Within six months his company had folded and he was declared bankrupt by the courts.

'There is only one alternative left,' he said to himself. 'I must become famous as a scholar. Then I shall be worthy of her love.' So he enrolled at the university and began to read for a degree. But, sadly, the boy was no better as a student than he had been as a soldier or a businessman. He failed his first-year exams with the lowest grades on record and was expelled from his college for academic incompetence.

In total self-despair he trudged wearily back to his home town. Years had passed and he had won no medals, gained no wealth, and earned no qualifications. He had been a failure at everything he had tried. 'I can never marry her now!' he sighed. 'I am not worthy of her love. Why, look at me! I'm poorer and less honoured now than I was when I left her. She'll never want a born loser like me. I shall just hide away in shame somewhere and hope that she thinks I'm dead.'

But as he entered the city, the count's daughter saw him from her father's palace window. She had heard of all his disappointments, but her love for him was still as strong as ever. Joyfully, she sped down the stairs and into the street to greet him.

'It's no good!' he wailed as he saw her. 'You can't still want to marry me. I'm not worthy of your love.'

'But I do want to marry you,' she said. 'I've always wanted to marry you. Look at your hand!'

There on his finger, worn, and so tight that he couldn't remove it, was the ring she had given him when they made their childhood vow.

'I promised to marry you,' she reminded him. 'Nothing you've done or failed to do can alter that. As far as I'm concerned a promise is a promise.'

It is important to understand that real love is not a tribute but a promise. '"Wilt thou take this woman to be thy wedded wife?" The man shall answer, "I will."' That's what love is – a voluntary, personal commitment to somebody.

When we say 'I will', we don't mean: 'I think you're the most attractive person in the world', or 'I reckon you've got the sharpest intelligence in the world', or 'I admire your heroism, your cooking, your athleticism, your temperament,' or whatever. No doubt there will be aspects and qualities of the person of which we do think highly, but then that is true of almost anybody. Rather, when we say 'I will', we are not fundamentally paying the other person a compliment, but expressing a personal commitment. We are making a promise; that's what love is.

It is such a hard lesson to learn, and there are some who never learn it. They are so insecure, so lacking in self-esteem, that they must be for ever seeking to earn the affection and respect of others. Like the young man in my fairytale, they are obsessed with the need to prove themselves worthy, and like him they never succeed. A depressing sense of failure and inadequacy haunts them all their lives. It's tragic, for happiness is often so close to their grasp, yet they dare not seize it till they feel they deserve it. And that of course they never do. If only they could learn that love is not a tribute but a promise; that happiness comes not from the struggle to prove our worthiness to anyone, but from the assurance of knowing that someone loves us just as we are, warts and all.

Some people who never learn that lesson cannot form secure relationships for that reason. Like the shoemaker's son, they cannot love because they dare not trust. I want to suggest that that is true not only of relationships between the sexes. It is true also of that supreme relationship between us human beings and God, of which all other personal relationships are but feeble echoes.

In the final section of the third chapter of his letter to the Galatians, Paul is spelling out for us a simple yet utterly fundamental lesson. We do not experience the love of God as a result of proving ourselves worthy of it. We discover that love as a free gift of God's grace, when we are humble enough to believe his promise.

For God has made a promise too, just like that daughter of the count. It is a vow of everlasting love, an indissoluble commitment. It is an irrevocable promise. In short, it is a *covenant*. That's the Bible's word for it. God made this covenant thousands of years ago with a man called Abraham. But as he stated plainly at the time, it wasn't just for Abraham's benefit alone. It was for everyone. 'All nations will be blessed through you,' God told him. Yet the extraordinary thing is that rather than believe that promise and depend upon it, the human race has been obsessed, just like the shoemaker's son, with proving that it is worthy of such divine love. To use the vocabulary of the apostle Paul, we have sought to establish our own righteousness, and we have tried to justify ourselves through works.

But Christianity isn't a religion of works like that at all. As in our story of the cobbler and the count's daughter, it is a relationship based on a promise. And it's a good job it is. For if we had to depend on our moral deserts for our salvation, heaven would be a very empty place.

'What you have got to realize is this,' Paul is saying. 'The love of God is not something we deserve, but something we receive. It isn't a tribute God pays to our moral achievement, or a reward, or a compliment. It is a promise. God had made a vow, and nothing we do or fail to do can alter that vow. As far as God is concerned, a promise is a promise.'

> Brothers, let me take an example from everyday life. Just as no-one can set aside or add to a human covenant that has been duly established, so it is in this case . . . What I mean is this: The law, introduced 430 years later, does not set aside the covenant previously established by God and thus do away with the promise. For if the inheritance depends on the law, then it no longer depends on a promise; but God in his grace gave it to Abraham through a promise (3:15, 17–18).

Anyone who has ever bought or sold a house knows how critical that day is when the solicitor tells you he has exchanged contracts. For until that day, the transaction is still uncertain. You may have a gentlemen's agreement on it, but either party can still back out of the deal without penalty. Once contracts have been signed and exchanged, however, a legally enforceable promise has been made from which there is no easy escape. Both parties are bound by the terms of the contract and it can't be changed.

Paul is alluding to something like that in verse 15. The

word 'covenant' in the secular usage of his day often meant what we would call a 'last will and testament'. That, of course, is another example of a legally binding document, the terms of which, like a contract, cannot be altered once it is signed, sealed and delivered.

If that is true of human covenants, argues Paul to the Galatians, it is even more true of the divine covenant. God made a promise to Abraham and nothing can possibly change it. It is irrevocable, immutable, inviolable. Whatever reason God had for giving the law, then, it must be consistent with the promise to Abraham and therefore may not be interpreted by the Judaizers in any fashion that undermines that promise.

There are, in fact, according to Paul, several things about the way the law was given which clearly indicate that it is fundamentally different from the promise and secondary to it.

For a start, there is that point, mentioned earlier, about the law being a conditional arrangement. If you keep it, you get the blessing, whereas the promise had no conditions attached at all (3:18).

More than that, the law was a bilateral agreement negotiated through intermediaries, whereas the promise was a unilateral deposition given directly to Abraham by God himself (3:19–20).

But most significant of all, there is the question of timing. The promise came first. All right, half a millennium after Abraham's death, God gives Moses the Ten Commandments. But that doesn't change the covenant. It can't. It doesn't even add a codicil to it.

All ways round, then, it is clear that the law of Moses and the promise to Abraham are fundamentally different kinds of arrangement. An obvious question to ask is: are they then incompatible with one another? Do they represent mutually contradictory religious ideas?

There have been plenty of Christians over the years who have drawn that conclusion. But it is important to notice that Paul refuses to go that far.

> Is the law, therefore, opposed to the promises of God? Absolutely not! For if a law had been given that could impart life, then righteousness would certainly have come by the law (3:21).

You could be forgiven, after all the negative things Paul has said about the Old Testament law, for anticipating the answer 'yes' to our question. But Paul refuses to drive the wedge between law and promise that deep. They are different, but not incompatible.

The point to realize is that the law was never intended to create the possibility of a relationship with God, for the promise had already done that. The law's job was altogether different. Fail to grasp that, and you are in danger of setting the law against the promise, and thus misunderstanding God's dealings with us human beings altogether.

The next question then is: what was the purpose the law? Paul himself anticipates it in 3:19, and his answer is crucial to the whole argument of this letter. It is this: the law was never intended to save us; it was given to prepare the way for a Saviour.

> What, then, was the purpose of the law? It was added because of transgressions until the Seed to whom the promise referred had come (3:19).

That word 'Seed' is a reference back to verse 16 and the terms of the promise to Abraham. God said, you recall, that Abraham's seed would be the source of blessing for the whole world. Paul sees significance in the singular noun, 'seed', as opposed to 'seeds'. That's a hint, he says, that the seed in question is not the Jews (plural) but one Jew in particular: the Seed of the promise; that is, the Messiah, the Christ.

The law was given, then, not to replace the promise or to change it, but to prepare the way for its fulfilment; to prepare the way for Jesus.

How did the law achieve that purpose? This is where Paul's argument is particularly compressed. But the two key phrases are in verses 19 and 24. Paul tells us in verse 19 that the law was added 'because of transgressions', and in verse 24 that it was 'put in charge to lead us to Christ'. The basic idea that seems to be in Paul's mind in both cases is that of preparatory education. Look at it this way. How would you explain a bicycle to an aborigine who had no word for 'wheel'? Or how would you explain a rainbow to a congenitally blind person who had no experience of colour? All communication requires an association between words and ideas. It is the purpose of early education to establish those associations.

Paul points out that the Old Testament law was all about providing us with a similar preparatory education in the things of God. This, of course, is why it is so important for us to study the Old Testament ourselves.

Some Christians think they can do without the Old Testament altogether. They read the New Testament, but they don't even possess a copy of the Old. From Paul we learn that you cannot understand the New Testament without the necessary hermeneutical tools and theological vocabulary provided by the Old. The Old Testament constitutes our biblical ABC. Only there shall we discover the elementary ideas without which we simply shall not be able to make sense of what the New Testament wants to teach us about Jesus.

In verse 24, Paul uses an interesting Greek word in that connection: *paidagōgos*, 'pedagogue'. The old Authorized Version translated it, 'the law was our schoolmaster'. But that is a slightly misleading rendering, because a pedagogue was not an academic tutor in the modern sense. He was a highly trusted slave who was put in charge of his master's son, rather like an old English nanny. He took the boy to classes, taught him his manners, made sure he did his homework, and when necessary tanned his hide! The education he imparted, therefore, was not academically very advanced, but it was a vital preparation for adult life. The pedagogue taught the boy his moral and social ABC, the elements of good behaviour and personal responsibility.

'Well,' points out Paul, 'just such a task of preliminary education was necessary for us too if we were ever to be safely entrusted with the fulfilment of that ancient promise to Abraham.' And that is what the Old Testament law is all about. It teaches us two things.

1. The law teaches us the reality of sin

That, I think, is at least part of what Paul is getting at by that terse phrase 'because of transgressions' (3:19). The law defined sin as 'transgression', that is, the breach of a moral boundary. To a limited extent it also restrained sin by its sanctions. Most important of all, it exposed sin to our private consciences – not merely as a catalogue of isolated blots on our moral record, but as an inner corruption that permeates our minds and hearts, frustrating our efforts even on those occasions when we want to do the right thing. The law makes it clear to us not just that we are sinners, but, as Paul puts it in verse 22, that 'the whole world is a prisoner of sin'.

This function of the law as the definer, restrainer and exposer of sin is still of great relevance today, of course. In the last few years there has been a huge amount of concern in the media over the decay of moral values in our society, particularly among the young. The murder of the toddler Jamie Bulger by two ten-year-old boys did much to sensitize us to this issue. The more recent killing of headmaster Philip Lawrence outside his school gates has further alerted us to the emergency that is developing. Now, scarcely a month passes without a leading article in our newspapers demanding some urgent answer to the need for moral education.

How do Christians respond to this anxiety? One response, of course, is evangelism. If people found Christ in great numbers, then a powerful moral dynamic would be unleashed in our culture that would transform public conduct in the way that, historically, the revivals did in the eighteenth century.

But what if revival doesn't come? Do we Christians have nothing to say to a secular society in its unbelief? I believe we do. According to Paul in this chapter, God was active in Israel long before the arrival of the gospel in Christ. The law of God was, at least in part, a temporary remedy given to the world 'because of transgressions'. Law cannot save us, it is true, but its moral education can do society an immense amount of good. And without that moral education, the good seed of the gospel is likely to fall on unprepared and spiritually hardened ground. For what is the point of telling people that Jesus saves, if their seared consciences feel no awareness of the sin from which they need to be saved?

2. The law teaches us our need of a Saviour

The Scripture declares that the whole world is a prisoner of sin, so that what was promised, being given through faith in Jesus Christ, might be given to those who believe (3:22).

Here is the crunch issue. Rules, like a strict governess, rebuke our moral failure and lock us in our room as punishment. But rules have no power to make us any better. Law can only show us our mistakes and penalize us for them. Like a copy of the penal code in the hands of a murderer, it can condemn, but it offers no hope of salvation, no hope at all. Hence the metaphor of the gaoler: 'We were held prisoners [not just by sin but] by the law' (3:23).

Ironically, however, that was God's very purpose in giving the law: not that we should try to establish our own righteousness by means of it, but that we might discover the helplessness of our moral plight and admit our desperate need of rescue. Where are we to look for that deliverance? Why, to the promise, of course.

Before this faith came, we were held prisoners by the law, locked up until faith should be revealed. So the law was put in charge to lead us to Christ that we might be justified by faith (3:23–24).

How does the coming of Jesus change our situation? Paul has already spelt out the answer:

61

Christ redeemed us from the curse of the law by becoming a curse for us, for it is written: 'Cursed is everyone who is hung on a tree.' He redeemed us in order that the blessing given to Abraham might come to the Gentiles through Christ Jesus, so that by faith we might receive the promise of the Spirit (3:13–14).

Frankly, these two verses are among the most important in this whole letter. Paul is telling us why the cross is so central to Christianity.

The law and the cross

If Christianity were just a religion of rules, a code of conduct, the cross of Jesus would necessarily be a marginal and dispensable item in its creed. You could see the cross, I suppose, as a model of the sacrificial obedience that the religious life demands. Or you could treat it, perhaps, as a kind of moral influence which, by its emotional power, motivates us to live the religious life. There have been plenty of people who have chosen to interpret the cross in just that kind of way. Indeed, as long as we think of Christianity as just a religion of rules, like other religions, some such conclusion is inevitable. The cross can be nothing but a powerful religious symbol or example to help us keep the rules.

Paul, however, is here affirming that the cross is much more than that. Indeed, far from encouraging religious rules, he is telling us that the cross actually delivers us from them. It is not intended as an incentive to law-keeping, but as the solution to our law-breaking. The purpose of the cross is to change not how *we* feel about our sins, but how

God feels about them. It is not a means of subjective influence on us, but an act of substitutionary sacrifice for us.

The law itself says that to hang the body of an executed criminal in public was a sign of execration. Such a person was under the curse of God. Yet Jesus, God's Messiah, hung in just such a shameful manner before the contempt of the world. Why? Why should God allow such an appalling thing to be done to his Son? Such a humiliation? Such a miscarriage of justice?

The answer is as exciting as it is shocking. On that cross he became 'a curse for us' (3:13). Like a man who takes his friend's place on the scaffold, so Jesus discharged our moral debt to the law of God on our behalf. He bore the curse of the broken law for us.

The scandal of the cross

Perhaps you're saying to yourself, 'Can Paul be serious? Can he really expect me to accept such a scandalous idea? Let me get this straight, Paul. You are saying that God is willing to accept cursed sinners because Jesus hung on the cross and bore the curse in their place? What kind of divine justice is that, which can acquit the guilty by victimizing the innocent? It is to attribute to the court of heaven a more monstrous corruption than that of the court of Pontius Pilate! At least Pilate resented the crowds when they clamoured for the death of the innocent Jesus so that the guilty Barabbas could be set free. But you, Paul, are suggesting that God planned the cross as just such a judicial exchange on a cosmic scale.'

Little wonder that the philosopher A. J. Ayer regarded

Christianity as the worst of all religions, because, he said, it rested on the idea of redemption through substitutionary sacrifice, an idea 'intellectually contemptible and morally outrageous'.

How would Paul have responded to that objection? I think I know the answer, but to find it we have to glance forward to the passage we shall be looking at in our final chapter. In 4:4 Paul tells us that the one God sent to this earth to redeem us was 'his Son'. People who object to Paul's explanation of the cross do so because they think he is portraying God as a spiteful, heavenly monster who punishes an innocent third party in order to satisfy his own ruthless lust for revenge. They imagine God to be like a Nazi commandant in the Second World War, executing innocent civilians in occupied France in response to the 'crimes' of the resistance movement. But that is a travesty of what Paul is saying, for a very simple reason. As far as God is concerned, Jesus is not a third party. Of course, God could not have taken some innocent person and arbitrarily made him or her carry the curse for a sinful world. That would indeed have been morally outrageous. But Jesus was not just any innocent person. Jesus was 'his Son'.

I don't pretend to be able to explain the mysteries of the Trinity and the incarnation. But the Bible insists that in an utterly real and profound sense God was 'in Christ', and that it was God himself, therefore, who hung on the cross.

When Christians look at the cross, then, they don't just see an example to which they must try to conform, or a moral influence to which they must try to respond. They see God himself, in the person of his Son, taking upon himself the curse pronounced by his own covenant law!

That is the fundamental reason Christianity is not and cannot be a religion of rules. Of course, it has a system of ethics. Paul will talk about those later, in chapters 5 and 6. He will even find a place for the Old Testament law, understood in the right way. But, at its root, Christianity isn't a matter of rules, for rules represent something we human beings do out of duty to God. Christianity is about something God had done out of love for us. On the cross, Christ redeemed us to open up the way for the Gentiles to enter into the blessing given to Abraham.

- He has solved the problem of that unkeepable law.
- He has fulfilled Habakkuk's prophetic vision.
- He has inaugurated the new age of the Spirit.

And he did all this for us, without our even lifting a finger.

Returning to rules

What the cross requires of us, then, is not a religion of rules, but a life of faith: a faith like Abraham's, that trusts God's promise and walks in the light of it. Frankly, Paul finds it hard to believe that anybody who has been told about the cross could possibly get enmeshed in a religion of rules all over again. But that, it seems, is what the Galatians were in danger of:

> You foolish Galatians! Who has bewitched you? Before your very eyes Jesus Christ was clearly portrayed as crucified (3:1).

'Someone must have put a magic spell on you,' Paul exclaims. 'How else could you have reverted to your old spiritual blindness?'

But it does happen. I have watched it happen with Christians who begin with a profound experience of salvation by God's free grace and a deep appreciation of the meaning of the cross. Yet with the passing of time, and maybe under the influence of other Christians, they become more and more legalistic.

It's no wonder that the man and woman in the street complain that Christianity is just a lot of do's and don'ts. For a great many professing Christians, that is exactly what it is.

- Thou shalt have thy daily quiet time.
- Thou shalt not wash thy car on Sunday.
- Thou shalt not enter a public house except as a member of an evangelistic team.
- Thou shalt not approach closer than a distance of 50 cms to any member of the opposite sex thou dost not intend to marry.
- Thou shalt be against abortion, divorce, evolution, Sunday trading and Communism.
- Thou shalt be for capital punishment, and religious education in schools.

Don't misunderstand me. Many of these things are perfectly defensible. I would hope that every Christian would set aside time regularly for God. I would hope that every Christian was pro-life. I would hope that every Christian would keep Sunday special. But the trouble is that so many of us assess a person's spirituality by these kinds of criteria. That is not Christianity at all, but just legalism in a new dress. Jesus died on the cross to redeem us from rules, not to put us in bondage to new ones.

What should we then learn from Paul's argument in this

passage about the irrevocable promise? We should learn that Christianity is not about rules, but about God's grace. It is about a relationship, and a promise.

Let me include a word on this score especially to those who, like me, are often troubled by feelings of failure. Could it be that you are spiritually in the same condition as that shoemaker's son? You want to call yourself a Christian, but only if you can prove yourself worthy of such a title. So you go to church, but only out of duty. You say your prayers, but only out of habit. You live a morally respectable life, but only for the sake of your reputation. Just like that shoemaker's son, all that really matters to you is your self-esteem. You want to be a Christian and keep your pride. But it doesn't work.

Maybe you are more successful at keeping your pride than the shoemaker's son was. Some people are, of course. Maybe you are admired by others for your moral upright-ness and your churchmanship. But inside, like the shoe-maker's son, you know what a failure you really are. You know that what others see is mere cant and hypocrisy. You know that when it comes to facing God on the last day, you won't feel 'worthy' at all. You'll feel like a worm! Maybe deep down inside you there is a profound anxiety, even a sense of despair, that all your attempts at worthiness have really achieved very little.

Learn from Paul's letter to the Galatians that legalism is a spiritual dead-end. Christianity is not about rules, but about a promise. God offers his covenant to you. Failure though you are, you can know that he loves you and will never give you up.

Give up on rules, then, and put your trust in God's promise.

3

An inalienable freedom

Galatians 3:26 – 5:12

It is for freedom that Christ has set us free.
Stand firm, then, and do not let yourselves be
burdened again by a yoke of slavery (5:1).

It is sad when a person knows enough about God to fear him, but not enough to love him. But that, I regret to say, is the plight of very many people in this world – religious people, even people who would call themselves Christians, yet whose faith suffices only to render them miserable and guilt-ridden.

Religion as bondage

Martin Luther was like that before his conversion. A scrupulously conscientious monk, he would regularly spend many hours in prayer. Yet no glimmer of joy ever illuminated that devotional discipline. Rather, he tells us, he lived in terror of God.

The story of John Wesley is not dissimilar. The son of a clergyman, he went up to Oxford to study to become a clergyman himself. There, with his brother Charles, he formed the so-called 'Holy Club', a group which quickly earned the derision of their fellow scholars for the fanatical enthusiasm of their religion. They gave them the nickname 'Methodists', because they were so methodical in their spiritual discipline. Yet as John Wesley looked back on those days from the perspective of his later experience, he wrote in his journal: 'I had then only the faith of a servant, not that of a son.'

That observation, I think, really hits the nail on the head. An enormous number of people in this world experience religion as a form of bondage: bondage to guilt, to superstition, to ritual and, most of all, a bondage to rules, a burdensome list of do's and don'ts.

Such religion restricts and burdens people, as Wesley put it, feeling more like the relationship of a servant to his master than of a child to his parent.

Nobody, I suspect, knew more about that kind of religion than Paul. For, like Luther and Wesley, he had begun life in the context of an obsessive, puritanical zeal. He was a Pharisee, and in first-century Judaism you couldn't get more religious than that! Fundamentalist in their theology, and perfectionist in their morality, the Pharisees represented Judaism in its most rigorous form. Yet it is clear from what Paul tells us about his own religious experience that Pharisaism imprisoned him. It taught him enough about God to make Paul fear him, but not enough to love him. As a result he found himself trapped on a treadmill of pedantic and anxiety-ridden religiosity. 'The faith of a servant', Wesley had called it. In Paul's judgment he could just as well have said 'of a slave'.

Then came that famous day when Paul discovered it didn't have to be like that. Religion could be a liberating experience, a deliverance from guilt, superstition, ritual and rules, instead of a bondage to all these things. The key to that spiritual emancipation was Jesus Christ, who had come to set people free. Paul experienced that freedom and it thrilled him to the bone. The consuming passion of his life quickly became sharing that freedom with others, such as these young believers in Galatia. And that is why, of course, he is so distressed by the news that a party of Jewish Christians with decidedly Pharisaical leanings had infiltrated the young churches of Galatia and was seeking to rebuild the prison walls of religious bondage. 'It isn't enough simply to believe in Christ,' they said. 'The Bible says that if you are to be saved you must contract into the covenant of Abraham. And that means you must be circumcised and keep the Jewish law.'

Paul was outraged. Such views were a denial of everything he stood for, and these Judaizers knew it. They were deliberately seeking to put a different gospel in the place of the one Paul taught. If they succeeded in their campaign, and propagated their revisionist theology of law, then the gospel of God's grace would be lost. Christianity in Galatia would become indistinguishable from a Jewish sect, and just as much a bondage to wearisome rules as the Pharisaism in which Paul had languished so painfully and for so long. He was determined to put a stop to it, and this letter to the Galatians is his attempt to do so.

Religion as racialism

In chapters 1 and 2, Paul began by defending the special authority of his apostolic teaching. People, he argued, can't go around preaching any message they like and calling it Christianity. The gospel is not man-made, but divinely inspired. Those who distort it bring a curse down on their heads. In chapter 3, Paul began to target specific aspects of the Judaizing false teaching that was gaining ground in the Galatian churches. We saw that in chapters 3 and 4 Paul marshalled four arguments against legalism, the view that you must earn salvation by obeying the Jewish law. In the last of these he demonstrated that the law of Moses, properly understood, was never intended to save people. The purpose of the law was rather to be a temporary guardian to the people of God until the time arrived when God's covenant promises were fulfilled.

Paul is still developing that final argument in Galatians 3:26 – 5:12. But as he does so, he increasingly fixes his sights not only on the legalism of the Judaizers, but also on their *racialism*. They believed that there were basically two kinds of people in the world: Jews and the rest. The Jews were morally and spiritually superior to everyone else, an ethnic élite uniquely blessed by God. Those who wanted to enjoy God's favour, therefore, had effectively to become Jews, that is, to observe the cultural distinctives laid down in the Jewish law, especially (for the men) circumcision. For Paul, such racialism was just as bad as their legalism, and both were completely incompatible with the Christian gospel.

He begins to draw out this particular aspect of the Christian message as he shares with us, from 3:26 onwards, the triumphant news that the time of promise-fulfilment has indeed come – and, with it, freedom!

A new family feeling

You are all sons of God through faith in Christ Jesus,
for all of you who were baptised into Christ have
clothed yourselves with Christ. There is neither Jew nor
Greek, slave nor free, male nor female, for you are all
one in Christ Jesus. If you belong to Christ, then you
are Abraham's seed, and heirs according to the promise
(3:26–29).

One of the things clothes did for you in Paul's day, as
indeed in ours, was to define your social status. How you
dressed told people what sex you were. It also told them
your age; for instance, a Roman boy exchanged his striped
tunic for a plain white one when he became an adult. Your
clothes also betrayed your rank; for instance, important
Roman men wore a toga with a purple border, whereas
slaves wore only rough, unrefined garments. But perhaps
most significant of all in the ancient world, your clothes
revealed your racial origin. Different people-groups had
different styles of national dress. All in all, a glance at the
clothes people wore told an enormous amount about them.

'When you became Christians', Paul says in 3:27 to the
Galatians, 'you were all given the same set of clothes, for
you were all clothed with Christ. Since that moment all the
old distinctions of social status and ethnic origin that used
to divide you have been masked by a new identity, that of a
child of God.'

It is important not to misunderstand Paul here. He is
not, of course, suggesting that Christianity completely
obliterated the cultural distinctives of Jewish and Greek
society. Christianity has no ambition to homogenize
everyone. It is obvious from the New Testament that Jews

73

were still Jews in the church, and Greeks were still Greeks; indeed, slaves were still slaves, masters were still masters, men were still men and women were still women! But a new group identity had been created that overlapped all that social diversity and generated an unprecedented unity within it.

It is hard for those of us who have been raised in a liberal western tradition to realize how radical this new unity in Christ is for Paul. A familiar Hebrew prayer of his day invited the pious Jewish man to thank God that he had not been born 'a Gentile, a slave, or a woman'! In all probability Paul had used that prayer himself in his pre-Christian days. It may even have been at the back of his mind as he wrote 3:28.

If so, the words of that prayer now stuck in his throat. Racial, class or sexist prejudice had no place in the new community of Jesus Christ. The experience of divine grace had levelled all believers down to the shared humility of children presented with a gift. That's one reason Paul is so angry with these Judaizers in Galatia, of course. For they were trying to perpetuate these social distinctions. They wanted to retain circumcision, an initiation rite that left a visible mark in a man's flesh, identifying him as a Jew. But with the coming of Christ, circumcision had become redundant. The mark of the Christian community was baptism, an initiation that left no visible mark in the flesh and that identified both men and women as Christian believers, and nothing else.

'Those Judaizers want to make out that Jews are special because they are the children of Abraham,' argues Paul. 'But I tell you, they are not special, not any longer. If you belong to Christ, then you are Abraham's children, and heirs of the covenant promise. As a result, you ought to feel a spiritual solidarity with one another as Christians that completely transcends the kind of social distinctions that the Judaizers want to maintain. You ought to feel like family.'

Is this true in the church today?

Someone from an ethnic minority might be saying privately, 'No racism among Christians? It doesn't feel like that in my church!' A young person who has just left school at sixteen might be thinking, 'No class prejudice among Christians? It didn't feel like that when I tried to talk to that Oxbridge student yesterday.' A woman might be saying, 'No sexism among Christians? Don't make me laugh! You should have seen my pastor's face when I asked why we never saw any female faces at the front of the church on Sundays!'

If we are honest, we have to admit that the kind of social discrimination that the Judaizers wanted is all too obvious among Christians today. That is another reason this letter to the Galatians is so relevant to us.

A new filial freedom

What I am saying is that as long as the heir is a child, he is no different from a slave, although he owns the whole estate. He is subject to guardians and trustees until the time set by his father. So also, when we were children, we were in slavery under the basic principles of the world. But when the time had fully come, God sent his Son, born of a woman, born under law, to redeem those under law, that we might receive the full rights of sons (4:1–5).

In the good old days, a twenty-first birthday party really meant something. That was the day you became, in the eyes of the law, a full citizen. You could now vote, marry without parental consent, and serve on a jury. You were, as they used to say, given the key of the door. You were no longer a child who couldn't be trusted, but an independent adult.

All that has gone. There is little special about reaching the age of twenty-one now except perhaps the size and price of the birthday cards. And that is a pity for our purposes, because it makes it a little harder to feel the full impact of the analogy Paul is drawing in these opening verses of chapter 4.

Roman law recognized a definite age when a young man attained his majority. Often it was at fourteen years, though there seems to have been some flexibility in the matter. A Roman father could, at his discretion, fix some other age if he wished. If a boy's father had died, then, during the period until he reached that appointed age of adulthood, he was placed under the supervision of someone called a tutor. Even though his father may have been a wealthy man, the boy couldn't touch a penny of his inheritance so long as the tutor had control of his affairs. As Paul puts it, he was no better off than a slave, even though technically he had title to the whole estate, for he was subject to the authority of 'guardians and trustees'. The two Greek words translated here broadly encompass the duties of a tutor: as *guardian*, he looked after the boy, and as *trustee*, he looked after his property. The boy remained in that situation of compulsory discipline and submission 'until the time set by the father' (verse 2), that is, until he legally came of age. Then, when that twenty-first birthday or its ancient equivalent at last arrived, everything changed overnight! At a stroke, the tutor was dismissed, the boy was free, and the inheritance was his to enjoy.

Paul is arguing here that something very similar has happened to the world at large. History is divided, in the mind of God, into two great epochs: a period of spiritual minority, followed by a period of spiritual majority. And these two epochs are separated by a single day: a kind of spiritual twenty-first birthday for the human race.

The age of minority

Let's think about the earlier period first, 'when we were children' (3:3). At that time, just like a Roman boy under a tutor, according to Paul, we were as good as slaves, even though, if we had only known it, our future destiny was noble and royal.

To what were we enslaved? That's where Paul's language gets a little complicated. He says in verse 3 that we were enslaved to 'the basic principles of the world'. What does he mean by that? We may well ask. There has been no small debate among the scholars on the point! The difficulty centres around the phrase 'basic principles', a translation of the single, rather fascinating, Greek word *stoicheia*.

Stoicheia has several related strands of meaning, but basically it means the 'fundamentals' of something. It could be used, for instance, of a child learning the alphabet, the 'ABC', as we would say. In fact the New Testament uses the word in exactly that fashion in Hebrews 5:12, when it speaks of the 'elementary truths of God's Word'. *Stoicheia* could also mean the fundamental constituents of the material universe – what we would call the chemical elements. It is used in that way in 2 Peter 3:10, where the writer speaks of the elements being destroyed by fire at the end of the world. But *stoicheia* could have a third shade of meaning too. It could refer to the fundamental forces in the spiritual world – that is, demons, angels and the like. The Greeks used it in this sense to speak of cosmic astrological deities which, some of them believed, controlled the destiny of the world.

The big question is: in what sense is Paul using the word here? The most obvious answer seems to be that he is using it in the first sense. The idea of learning your ABC fits in very well with what he has been saying about a child growing up under a tutor. In fact, as we saw in looking at 3:24–25, Paul compared the function of the Old Testament law to that of a pedagogue who was responsible for a Greek boy's early education and discipline. If we link this passage in chapter 4 with that final paragraph of chapter 3, it seems certain that at least one of these *stoicheia*, which Paul says hold the world in bondage during the period of its spiritual minority, must be the law. As he put it in 3:23: 'We were held prisoners by the law, locked up until faith should be revealed.'

But there is more to it than that, for Paul writes:

> Formerly, when you did not know God, you were slaves to those who by nature are not gods. But now that you know God – or rather are known by God – how is it that you are turning back to those weak and miserable principles? Do you wish to be enslaved by them all over again? (4:8–9).

The word 'principles' is once again a translation of *stoicheia*. But Paul cannot be referring to the Old Testament law this time, for he is speaking directly to the Galatians, who were pagans, not Jews, before they became Christians. 'They were slaves,' he argues, not to the law, for they didn't know it, but to 'those who by nature are not gods'. In other words, the Christians in Galatia were trapped in the worship of pagan idols. Yet clearly these false deities, in Paul's mind, also belong to the general category of the 'basic principles', or *stoicheia*, that imprisoned the human race in the pre-Christian era.

The implications of this are rather startling. As we have seen, the leading characteristic of the earlier period (which we have called the world's spiritual minority) is bondage. Paul insists that this is so whether we are Jews or Gentiles. The only difference our cultural background makes is what holds us in bondage.

For some, like the Jews, that bondage is to religious rules. Ironically, the law which God gave as a guardian, to provide moral education and to limit the extent of evil in society arising from our sinful rebellious natures, becomes a cruel tyrant that holds us in chains of guilt and condemnation.

For others, such as the Galatians, that bondage is to pagan philosophy and religion. The spiritual instinct that generates such metaphysical speculation is, like the Old Testament law, God-given. Human beings ask questions about ultimate meaning, and devise religions for themselves, because they possess an innate awareness of God and the mystery of existence. But, just as our human sinfulness turns God-given law into legalistic bondage for the Jew, so it turns God-given spirituality into bondage to idolatry for the Greek.

All ways round, therefore, this earlier period of human history was characterized by slavery: slavery to the fundamental components of the old order of things, the *stoicheia* of a fallen world. Jewish law, pagan gods or human philosophy – the precise identity of our gaoler depends on how and where we are brought up. But, Jew or Gentile, enslaved is what we are.

This, of course, undermines the élitist pretensions of the Judaizers. They wanted to make out that to be a Jew was to be spiritually superior to a Gentile. But Paul insists that is not the case. Jew or Gentile, our natural condition is one of bondage – until the 'twenty-first birthday' of the human race at last arrived.

The age of majority

Notice Paul's great 'But': 'But when the time had fully come, God sent his Son' (4:4). Notice too the force of what Paul is now saying. Here is yet another insight into why those Judaizers were so woefully astray. They were living in the past, like theological dinosaurs. Paul is convinced that the age of our spiritual minority has ended. Its end was signalled the moment Jesus came into the world.

Observe that he came into the old world, the world that was still under the tutelage of rules. Jesus took our nature, sharing the heritage of our moral failure and our spiritual bondage. He was 'born of a woman, born under the law' (4:4). In every respect, then, he was a human being, just like us. As Paul puts it elsewhere, he was made 'in the likeness of sinful man' (Romans 8:3). There was only one difference. He didn't belong here. He had come from somewhere else. Like a commando parachuted behind enemy lines on a secret mission, so Jesus had been sent into the world by God.

His purpose? 'Redeem them!' Those were his Father's

orders. He was to redeem them from their slavery to the old order of things and from their bondage to the *stoicheia* of a fallen world, and to bring them into the liberty of the Father's new world, in which they will not be slaves any more, but sons and daughters of God.

It was no easy commission for Jesus to receive. For there was only one way a slave could be freed in the ancient world, and that was by the payment of a ransom price. Redemption was a costly business. So it was for Jesus. The law had a claim on us, for we were guilty of breaking it. The demonic spirits of wickedness had a claim on us, for we had served and worshipped them. The iron grip in which the *stoicheia* of the old age held us could be broken only if those claims were discharged, if those moral debts were cleared, and if those sins were atoned for. And that, therefore, is what Jesus had to do for us. Remember how Paul put it earlier: he 'redeemed us from the curse of the law by becoming a curse for us' (3:13).

That great deed of purchase on the cross results in God now giving us the key of the door. We are slaves to the old order of things no longer. A new era has begun, one in which we have received 'the full rights of sons'. For literally the word Paul uses in 4:5 is 'adoption'. By choosing that word, Paul is demonstrating that the title 'son' is no mere metaphor in this context. It has legal force. Just as an adopted son in Roman law had exactly the same rights as a natural son, so we may enjoy all the privileges of the children of God.

For, being justified by faith, we are no longer viewed by God as part of a rebellious creation. We are seen as part of his divine family. More than that, we are regarded as part of his adult family – sons and daughters who have come of age and are free to enjoy the heritage of liberty which is the advantage of their noble birth. That's why Paul could say: 'You are all sons of God through faith in Christ Jesus' (3:26). Now he can add:

> Because you are sons, God sent the Spirit of his Son into our hearts, the Spirit who calls out, '*Abba*, Father.' So you are no longer a slave, but a son; and since you are a son, God has made you also an heir (4:6–7).

Enjoying our inheritance

C. H. Spurgeon, the nineteenth-century preacher, tells a story which well illustrates how people's ideas of God get distorted by legalistic religion. He recounts how one of his fellow Baptist ministers went to the house of an elderly woman to give her the money for her rent as a gift from the church's poor-relief fund. He knocked again and again, but failed to get any answer. He discovered later that the old lady had been inside all the time. When he asked her to explain why she hadn't answered the door, she replied: 'Oh, I heard the knocking. But I thought it was the rent man come to evict me for what I owed!'

That is a parable of the ironic misunderstanding that keeps numerous people outside of Christ. We know we are accountable for our sins, so when we hear God knocking on the door of our hearts, we immediately jump to the conclusion that he has come as the rent man to claim that debt of moral obligation. Instead of opening our lives to him, we feign deafness like the old lady. We shut our ears to the invitation of God's Word, convinced that if we respond he will certainly make us regret it!

Such a misunderstanding is a tragedy. The truth is that

he knocks not as the ruthless rent man, demanding payment, but as the generous donor of charity, to provide it. It is the Saviour's knock we hear. But we are so ready to think it is the taskmaster's.

If that distorted perception is yours, let the beautiful things that are true of a child of God, recounted by Paul in this letter, sink deep into your consciousness.

We have, first, *a new nature*. 'God sent the Spirit of his Son into our hearts.' Human parents can give an adopted child a legal status, but they can't change its biological inheritance. God, however, actually shares his divine genes with his adopted children! As we shall see in the final chapter, that Spirit generates in us a new character, reflecting our new family likeness.

Secondly, we have *a new intimacy*. 'The Spirit . . . calls out, "*Abba*, Father."' Of course, it is possible for Christians to treat God with impertinent familiarity. But we can also fail to approach God with sufficient boldness and affection. The relationship the Spirit encourages within us is not remote or formal, but warm and spontaneous, like a child on the lap of a parent. Perhaps this is a special comfort to those who have no experience of a close and intimate relationship with their earthly parents. The gospel more than compensates us for our dysfunctional family backgrounds. What is more, it provides us with a Father who is not only very warm and loving, but also phenomenally rich!

Our Father gives us, thirdly, *a new destiny*. 'Since you are a son, God has made you also an heir.' The blessing of adoption doesn't stop with the Spirit. He is just the first instalment. There is an inheritance, too, to which we have incontestable title. Can you imagine the exhilaration a Roman boy from an aristocratic patrician family must have felt when he came of age and was able to roam through the acres of his father's estate as his own? Just think, then, how exhilarated we should feel at the prospect of being heirs of the universe!

Fourthly, we are granted *a new dignity*. 'So you are no longer a slave, but a son.' As we saw, John Wesley confessed, 'I had then the faith of a servant, not of a son.' There can be only one explanation for his words. Wesley was at that time living by the rule-book. He had not moved out of his spiritual infancy, been born again of the Spirit, been adopted into God's family, or discovered the vast honour which the King of the universe has bestowed on every Christian.

Is it possible to imagine that anyone who had once made that discovery could wish to go back to the status of a slave again? Is it possible to conceive of someone who had tasted freedom voluntarily seeking to return to bondage? Paul could hardly believe it, but that is exactly what the Galatians were close to doing!

A personal appeal

If you have ever been lost in a maze, you may have had that frustrating experience of walking for what seems like miles, only to rediscover the sweet-wrapper you discarded a few minutes after entering. In spite of all your investigation of the maze's pathways, you have ended up precisely where you started. Something like that had happened to these Galatians. Though there was no danger of their reverting to their old pagan idols, they were, nevertheless, in danger of turning the clock back to their pre-Christian past. For by flirting with the teaching of the Judaizers in their midst, as

Paul saw it, they were reverting to the religion of the old age:

> You are observing special days and months and seasons and years! I fear for you, that somehow I have wasted my efforts on you (4:10–11).

The exasperation in Paul's voice is evident as he complains: 'In the old days you saw special significance in certain days and months because of your superstitious belief in astrology and the signs of the zodiac. Now Jesus has delivered you from all that pagan superstition. But you are getting enmeshed instead, and similarly, in the sabbatarianism of the Jewish religious calendar!'

This is an extraordinary line for an ex-Pharisee like Paul to take. He is suggesting that there is no difference in principle between observing the Feast of Saturn as a pagan and observing the Feast of Tabernacles as a Jew. Both practices belong to the old order. 'You should be beyond such infantile games now,' he argues. 'Why, if you go along with what these Judaizers are saying, I might just as well have stayed in Antioch and never bothered preaching the gospel to you at all.'

It is not difficult to sense the note of personal injury in these verses. In the two paragraphs that follow, that note intensifies. Paul breaks off from his theological arguments to make a very direct appeal to friendship. The affection he felt for these Galatians shines through in phrases like 'I plead with you, brothers' (4:12) and 'my dear children' (4:19). He reminds them of the circumstances of their first meeting. He hadn't planned to visit Galatia at all, it seems. But an illness forced him to stop off in their region to recover. Superstitious people might easily have regarded that illness as a sign of divine disfavour or spiritual impotence. 'This Paul can't be much of a man of God if he is for ever getting sick!' they might have reasoned.

'But', asserts Paul, 'you didn't treat me with scorn or contempt in that way at all. You welcomed me instead as if I was an angel of God' (see verse 14). 'Why,' he adds, 'you would have given your own eyes to help me' (see verse 16 – a hint perhaps that the illness in question was an ophthalmic condition). 'What has become of that happy friendship between us now?' he asks. 'I am not harbouring any grudge against you, so why can't you behave in the same way towards me?' (see verse 12). 'Have I become your enemy,' he asks, 'simply because I speak to you straight from the shoulder about these Judaizers you seem so enamoured with? Is it that you love me only when I say what you want to hear?'

The most biting of all, however, are the sentiments of 4:17–18:

> Those people are zealous to win you over, but for no good. What they want is to alienate you from us, so that you may be zealous for them. It is fine to be zealous, provided the purpose is good, and to be so always and not just when I am with you.

Paul is probably using the verb 'to be zealous' here sarcastically, for those rival Judaizers may well have styled themselves 'zealots', as pious Jews often did in those days. If so, Paul's sarcasm has a punning edge to it, because the verb was also commonly used in the Greek world to speak of courting somebody's favour with ardent displays of attention. Verse 17 could therefore be paraphrased: 'These people are ingratiating themselves with you; they are insinuating themselves into your affections.'

'This is not because they are genuinely concerned for your best interests,' insists Paul. 'They just want to drive a wedge between us so that, isolated from my influence, you will become their private little group of sycophants, hanging on their every word. Their goal is that you finish up, in your simplicity, courting their affection, as they in their cunning have begun by courting yours. Can't you see you are being seduced, not sincerely wooed at all? There is nothing wrong with enthusiastic commitment to a teacher provided it's a wholesome and genuine relationship. We had such a relationship once. It would be nice if such loyalty could be relied upon in the teacher's absence as well as in his presence!'

Lest the sarcastic edge of that statement sounds too much like sour grapes, however, Paul hastens to stress that his purpose is not to engage in cheap emotional blackmail. He goes on, in effect, to say: 'I'm not writing in this way out of churlish pique. Unlike those Judaizers, my concern for you is utterly sincere. Right now I feel not so much like a jilted lover as an anxious parent!'

> My dear children, for whom I am again in the pains of childbirth until Christ is formed in you, how I wish I could be with you now and change my tone, because I am perplexed about you! (4:19–20).

There is an important lesson here for young Christians. Be discerning about those who want to influence your spiritual development. Zeal is not an infallible test of spirituality. There are far too many groups around, bearing the name of Christ, which are really parasites on the church, seducing young believers into their exclusive little legalistic clubs. You will find them knocking on your door, talking piously, behaving caringly, and obviously very keen! Maybe they will offer you a free magazine, or get their Bible out and quote so many texts that you will be spellbound at their erudition. Paul's personal appeal to the Galatians is also an appeal to you. Don't be credulous about their motives. Once they have sucked you into their cultish party machine, they will destroy your joy. They will drive a wedge between you and other Christians and arrest your spiritual development.

Given that we all need models when we are young in our faith, look for men and women of Paul's stamp as your mentors. They may not be able to give you as much time as others (Paul was a busy man). They may not appear as attractive or as powerful as others (Paul was often a sick man). They may not always speak the comfortable words you want to hear (Paul was an honest man). But, believe me, a person like Paul has one great advantage as a spiritual counsellor. He is not trying to mould you into a little plastic replica of himself, treating you like his own private ego trip. He does not create a dependency relationship that stifles your own opportunity for growth. Such a person's sole ambition is to see 'Christ formed in you'.

An argument from an Old Testament parallel

Tell me, you who want to be under the law, are you not aware of what the law says? For it is written that Abraham had two sons, one by the slave woman and the other by the free woman. His son by the slave woman was born in the ordinary way; but his son by the free woman was born as the result of a promise (4:21–23).

At this point, Paul launches into a most fascinating section of his letter. He has one more plank of theological argument to put in place in his discussion of the relationship between the covenant of Abraham and the law of Moses. It is fascinating because of the style of biblical interpretation which Paul uses to make his case.

Two ways in which Old Testament narrative may help a preacher to make a point need clarifying briefly to enable us understand what Paul is doing. First, *illustration*. In an illustration we compare two situations which, coincidentally, share some parallels. This helps to communicate an idea by analogy. For instance, Rahab tied a scarlet cord in her window as a sign of protection when the Israelites conquered Jericho (Joshua 2). Many a preacher has used that story as an illustration of the protective sign of Christ's blood. And there is no harm in such an illustrative use of the Old Testament story, provided we realize that the original author did not intend any such connection. The illustration adds nothing to the authority of what is being said about Christ's blood. It is merely a kind of verbal visual aid to help the preacher communicate. If the point he is making is erroneous, then no amount of illustrative stories, biblical or otherwise, will make it any truer.

A second way of using Old Testament narrative is called *typology*. In typology, too, there is a correspondence between the events of an Old Testament story and a spiritual New Testament meaning. But the distinctive thing about typology is that these correspondences are not purely coincidental. Typology works on the assumption that there is a pattern in God's dealing with people, and that God has intentionally woven that pattern into the story of the Old Testament so that we might recognize it and learn from it. Even though the inspired historian was unaware of any such meaning in his narrative, where a typological correspondence is identified, that meaning is nevertheless authoritative. It isn't just an illustration the preacher has chosen to use for his own convenience. It is part of the intention of God in the Bible passage concerned.

A word of caution: typology has been a happy hunting-ground for every kind of crackpot Christian. We need a very mature grasp of biblical theology before we can make responsible and reliable use of typology. Only the New Testament apostles can lay down the ground-rules for this kind of interpretation and define its proper boundaries. But there is no doubt that in the mind of Paul, typology is a legitimate way of looking at the Old Testament. For here in Galatians 4 he is exploiting it.

He tells us in verse 24 that he is speaking 'figuratively'. The Greek word he uses means 'allegory'. But that mustn't mislead us into thinking that Paul regards the Old Testament story to which he is referring as a fictional parable, like Bunyan's allegory *Pilgrim's Progress*. Clearly, he did not.

What Paul is arguing is that God's dealings with Hagar and Sarah are theologically analogous to his dealings with men and women generally. There is a typological correspondence between what happened to them, and certain New Testament truths. In fact, there are no fewer than four typological motifs that are explicitly or implicitly woven into these verses:

- two wives of Abraham: Sarah and Hagar
- two sons of Abraham: Isaac and Ishmael

- two mountains of the Middle East: Zion and Sinai
- two cities of Jerusalem: an earthly one and a heavenly one

It is not difficult to see that what these four typological pairs have in common in the number two! That may well be more than a trivial observation. I suspect that one of the reasons Paul embarks on this typological argument is that his opponents used the same method on the same Old Testament story to support their racialist ideas. 'There are two kinds of people in this world,' they maintained. 'There are the people of the covenant, the children of Sarah, represented by Isaac: namely, the Jews. And there are the people outside the covenant, the children of Hagar, represented by Ishmael: namely, the Gentiles. If you want to inherit the Promised Land, then, you had better join the race of Isaac!'

Paul has a typological interpretation of his own that turns these conclusions on their head. He insists that each of these pairs corresponds spiritually not to two races, but to two kinds of religion. On the one hand, there is a religion of bondage which characterizes the old covenant, represented by Hagar (who was, significantly, a slave woman), Ishmael, Sinai and the earthly city of Jerusalem. On the other hand, there is a religion of freedom which characterizes the new covenant, represented by Sarah (who most certainly was not a slave woman), Isaac, Zion and the heavenly city of Jerusalem. Paul argues that these two systems of religion have always been at odds with each other, just as Sarah and Hagar became rivals in Abraham's household, and the descendants of Isaac and of Ishmael have been at war in the Middle East ever since.

'But', says Paul, 'make no mistake about it. Whatever

their claims may be, it is those Judaizers in your midst who belong to Hagar, not the Gentiles. And it is we Christians who are the true heirs of Sarah and Isaac, not the Jews. As for the Promised Land, we belong to the real Jerusalem, which isn't located in Palestine at all, but in heaven.'

> Now Hagar stands for Mount Sinai in Arabia and corresponds to the present city of Jerusalem, because she is in slavery with her children. But the Jerusalem that is above is free, and she is our mother . . . Therefore, brothers, we are not children of the slave woman, but of the free woman (4:25–26, 31).

There are indeed two groups of people in this world, but the distinction between them has nothing to do with race, circumcision, or Jewish law. It has to do with faith in Christ. This typological line of reasoning would have dealt a devastating blow to the Judaizers in Galatia. Never before had they heard such a novel interpretation of their favourite Bible stories!

A final warning

> It is for freedom that Christ has set us free. Stand firm, then, and do not let yourselves be burdened again by a yoke of slavery (5:1).

Paul has at last reached the end of his long catalogue of arguments against the legalism and racialism of the Judaizers. Here, at the beginning of chapter 5, he is starting to pull together the threads of the previous two chapters.

'Legalism is a *burdensome* religion,' he says, 'a yoke of

slavery'. The picture is that of an ox being bowed down by a crippling weight across its shoulders. Pious Jews sometimes used this metaphor to describe their submission to the law of Moses, but Paul has no time for such religious masochism. Jesus said that his yoke was easy and his burden light (Matthew 11:30). Only fools would allow themselves to be encumbered again by a religion of onerous rules and regulations, once they had experienced release from such a burden.

Legalism is a *hopeless* religion, he continues.

> Again I declare to every man who lets himself be circumcised that he is required to obey the whole law (5:3).

To be a consistent legalist, you can't pick and choose which of Moses' requirements you're going to obey. If your aim is to satisfy the righteousness of God through obeying rules, you have to submit to every single one of them. As Paul argued in chapter 3, a 50% mark won't suffice to pass God's moral examination. He demands straight A's in every subject. Only a pompous idiot would dream that he could attain such an impossibly high standard.

Paul goes on to declare that legalism is an *apostate* religion.

> Mark my words! I, Paul, tell you that if you let yourselves be circumcised, Christ will be of no value to you at all . . . You who are trying to be justified by law have been alienated from Christ; you have fallen away from grace (5:2, 4).

The whole point of the Christian message is that we can't make ourselves right with God by our own efforts. If we could have done so, Jesus would not have needed to come. We could have climbed the ladder to heaven on our own. Rather, it was precisely because we were helpless and hopeless, condemned by God's law and unable to save ourselves from judgment, that he stepped in. By his death on the cross, he paid the penalty for our sin and made it possible for God to be merciful toward us. This is the gospel, a message of divine grace. Christ promises to vindicate before the bar of God's justice all those who bear the seal of his Spirit. He will enfold in the robe of his own matchless moral perfection all those united to him by faith.

> By faith we eagerly await through the Spirit the righteousness for which we hope (5:5).

Notice that word 'await'. We wait for this vindication. We don't earn it. Christ has promised it, and we simply rest on that word in the calm assurance that he who never lies will fulfil it.

The Jewish law, then, is irrelevant to the Christian. Whether a man is circumcised or not is irrelevant. The only thing that matters is the faith that links us to Jesus. Anybody who chooses to get circumcised, therefore, is effectively saying that he does not trust Jesus. He wants to be justified by the law instead. All that Jesus has done for a world of sinners is of no value to him at all. There is only one word for that: apostasy. Such people have 'fallen away from grace'.

It clearly comes as a shock to Paul to discover such apostasy within the Galatian congregations. He is alarmed and perplexed.

> You were running a good race. Who cut in on you and kept you from obeying the truth? (5:7).

'You've been tripped up in the Christian race,' he says. Just as it takes only a small quantity of yeast to permeate and raise a whole lump of dough, so it takes only one or two plausible demonic infiltrators to corrupt a church. But they won't get away with it! Paul is confident that the Galatian believers will see through the seduction, and that those responsible will be disciplined.

> I am confident in the Lord that you will take no other view. The one who is throwing you into confusion will pay the penalty, whoever he may be (5:10).

He has one final issue to deal with. It seems that his opponents were trying to discredit Paul by impugning his integrity. They suggested that he wasn't consistent on the circumcision issue. When it suited him, they jeered, he was willing to support the circumcision of Christian converts (such as Timothy in Acts 16, perhaps?). Paul is infuriated by this accusation, and refutes it with scorn and indignation.

> Brothers, if I am still preaching circumcision, why am I still being persecuted? In that case the offence of the cross has been abolished (5:11).

In other words, the whole reason these Jews hate the Christian message so much is that the cross of Christ renders their religion of rules redundant. It scandalizes them that Paul should preach salvation without the law. If he had changed his policy on that matter, they would have welcomed him back into the Judaistic fold with open arms. But they haven't done that, and they won't do that, because contrary to these libellous rumours, Paul declares, he has not changed his gospel. And as if to impress indelibly on the minds of his Galatians readers just how implacably hostile to this legalistic Judaism he was, he ends his diatriabe with an insult that, we must admit, comes close to vulgarity.

> As for those agitators, I wish they would go the whole way and emasculate themselves! (5:12).

There is a pun here, for the verb Paul is using can mean simply 'to cut off'. The verse could therefore be rendered, 'I wish these agitators would separate themselves from you.' But with the subject of circumcision so high on the agenda, it is impossible to imagine that the other common meaning of the verb was not also in Paul's mind, namely 'to castrate'. As one commentator has put it, Paul suggests that if these Judaizers are so fond of surgical operations like circumcision for religious motives, why don't they go the whole hog and imitate the pagan priests of Cybele, who make eunuchs of themselves!

Guard your freedom

From this section of the Galatian letter, then, we learn three main lessons:

- Christianity is meant to make us feel *free!* If we don't, something is wrong.
- We should beware the bondage of pressure groups that want to make us into clones of themselves.
- We must beware the bondage of evangelical pietism that tries to make us conform to a particular style of being Christian.

Many non-Christians have been put off church precisely because they don't find freedom there. They don't like the stereotyped image. They find the predictable clichés tiresome, and the sanctimonious attitudes repulsive. While they may be aware of some glimmering spiritual need in their souls, the last thing in the world they want to do is join that appalling God Squad!

Be reassured! We don't need to be like anyone except Jesus. He died on the cross to set us free. He does not demand that we wear a permanent evangelical grin. He does not expect us to mouth evangelical platitudes. He invites us to trust him. And we shall not find that relationship of trust stultifying. Religion says, 'Obey the rules!' 'Be like this!' But the message of this letter to the Galatians is that Christ has set us free, and we must never again submit to enslavement (5:1).

John Newton was a slave-trader in the eighteenth century. At the age of twenty-three he found Christ. He tells us that he strove never to allow the passing of the years to blur the memory of the new liberty that Christ had brought him. So above his mantelpiece he fastened this text:

> Thou shalt remember that thou wast a bondman [slave] in the land of Egypt, and the LORD thy God redeemed thee (Deuteronomy 15:15; 24:18, Authorized Version).

We Christians need to be determined to guard our freedom. Of course, freedom can be abused, as we shall see in our final chapter. Our freedom does not mean that we can live as we please. But let's remember that we are meant to feel free. Let no-one steal that sense of jubilant emancipation from us.

4

An inner war

Galatians 5:13 – 6:18

You see in me the one free man in the whole Roman Empire. You should be glad to have at least among you an emperor who points the way to freedom.

Those are the words of the Emperor Caligula, as portrayed in the play of the same name by the French author Albert Camus.

Freedom according to Caligula

Is Camus right? Did Caligula represent an archetypal freedom?

In one sense, he surely did. Of all the monarchs who have ever reigned, none has engaged in such wild caprice as he did. Power, for him, meant the complete absence of self-restraint, the total abdication of personal responsibility. No matter how cruel, disgusting and insane his impulses, Caligula was a man who did precisely as he pleased.

Many people would define freedom in similar terms. They see it as the capacity to do as you want, unconfined by restrictions imposed from outside. For the revolutionary it means political independence – freedom from unwelcome authority. For the capitalist it means economic *laissez-faire* – freedom from market controls. For the hippie it meant permissiveness – freedom from moral conventions. For existentialist philosophers such as Camus it meant something close to whimsicality – freedom even from the constraints of rationality and common sense.

That's why Caligula fascinated Camus so much. Here was a man who was not afraid to do his own thing, no matter how absurd or arbitrary. In fact, the more absurd and arbitrary, the better. Here, surely, was a truly free man whose power of choice was unfettered by anything.

But was he really free?

Even Camus had his doubts on this point, for his play ends with Caligula, in a momentary respite from his madness, addressing himself in a mirror: 'I have chosen a wrong path, a path that leads to nothing. My freedom isn't the right one . . .' In a final fit of rage and disillusionment, he hurls a stool at his own reflection before turning to face his assassins. It is the critical moment in the play, a window of truth thrown open briefly to illumine the folly of Caligula's original libertarian claims. He wasn't a free man at all. He was just a libertine.

Although the two concepts are utterly different, Caligula was not the first to muddle liberty and libertinism. 'Freedom' is a dangerous word precisely because it is so easily confused with licence. As someone has said: 'Oh freedom, what liberties are taken in thy name!'

Freedom, properly understood, is not the absence of all constraints upon our behaviour, but submission to the right constraints. It is not the rebellion that recognizes no authority, but the discernment that distinguishes legitimate authority. True freedom is not the licence to do as we please, but the liberty to do as we ought.

Our society badly needs to relearn that vital distinction. For anarchy is in the air today, whether it is manifested in the form of a terrorist bomb in Docklands, tree houses on the site of the Newbury bypass, animal-rights campaigners smashing up laboratories, or pro-life campaigners wrecking American abortion clinics. Our contemporary society is in danger of failing to observe the difference between exercising liberty and taking liberties.

Freedom according to Paul

Ultimately, of course, it all comes down to the issue of law. Does a framework of external rules necessarily spell the end of freedom? By Caligula's definition, of course, it does. But not by the apostle Paul's.

That may seem surprising. Paul has expressed profound reservation about rules throughout this letter to the Galatians. He has warned his readers again and again about bondage to law, culminating with that marvellous exhortation at the beginning of chapter 5: 'Stand firm, then, and do not let yourselves be burdened again . . .'

Yet, outspoken as the apostle's polemic against law has been, it is important not to get his call to freedom out of proportion. Paul has been countering a group of Judaistic false teachers who were trying to impose the law of Moses on Gentile Christians. His opposition to their ideas has indeed been vitriolic at times. But when Paul says, 'It is for freedom that Christ has set us free' (5:1), he is certainly not talking about the absolute, unqualified freedom represented by Camus' Caligula. Nothing could be further from the truth. Paul is no libertine, though that may well have been one of the accusations levelled against him by his rivals.

As we saw at the beginning of this book, these Judaizers were probably not just legalists, asserting that circumcision was necessary to salvation. They were also nomists, avowing that law was God's remedy for sin in the life of Christian. For nomists, obeying the law is what makes the people of God morally distinctive. They reckoned that by offering the Gentiles a law-free gospel, Paul was issuing an open invitation to moral anarchy, and imperilling the holiness of the church.

In this final section of the letter, Paul takes up that issue. He has dealt with the arguments of the legalists, who want to be justified by the law. Now he levels his theological gunsights on the nomists, who want to be sanctified by the law. His reply comprises three elements. He tells us, first, what freedom really means (5:13–15); secondly, what the Spirit of Christ does (5:16–23), and thirdly, what we must do (5:24 – 6:10).

What freedom really means

You, my brothers, were called to be free. But do not use your freedom to indulge the sinful nature; rather, serve one another in love. The entire law is summed up in a single command: 'Love your neighbour as yourself.' If you keep on biting and devouring each other, watch out or you will be destroyed by each other (5:13–15).

The nomists had a point. A perverse logic could twist Paul's gospel into an excuse for all kinds of permissive behaviour. Forgiveness is free, Paul declares. We're not under the law. Christ calls us to freedom. From this, we can surely deduce that we can live exactly how we want! Once we have bought our fire insurance, there's no reason why we shouldn't play with matches!

It is plain from these verses that such a conclusion would be utterly misplaced. To argue that way is to have the same understanding of freedom as Caligula. Paul understands it very differently. He tells us three things about Christian freedom that make that fact transparently clear.

What freedom is not

First, *Christian freedom does not mean lack of self-discipline*. 'Do not use your freedom to indulge the sinful nature.' Paul is using a military term, meaning a bridgehead or a launch-pad. Christian freedom must not be abused in such a way as to give opportunity to the base and self-centred side of human nature. It is not an excuse for a lack of self-discipline.

Secondly, *Christian freedom does not mean lawlessness*. 'The entire law is summed up in a single command.' How astonishing! Paul, who has spent so much time telling us how useless the law is, now quotes from Leviticus 19:18 without a murmur of apology or a hint of embarrassment! What can he be thinking of?

The issue is quite simple. Paul has never denied the value of the law as moral education. In fact, he insisted in Galatians 3 that moral education was its main purpose. If we want to know what kind of behaviour pleases God, it is to the law that we must look. Where has God revealed his righteous standards more clearly?

When Paul says we are free from the law, he does not mean that God has changed his mind about the difference between right and wrong. He means that we are delivered from the futile attempt to get right with God or stay right with him by means of the law. But as a revelation of God's moral standards the law can never be abrogated. That's why Jesus himself said, in the Sermon on the Mount, that it would be a mistake for anyone to think his mission was to abolish the law. Not an iota of the Old Testament, he insisted, had become irrelevant with his coming (Matthew 5:17–18). Indeed, Paul's comment about the law being summed up in Leviticus 19:18 comes very close to Jesus' own summary of the law when he quotes the same verse (see Matthew 22:37–40).

The law is useless, then, as a source of moral salvation or moral power, but it is indispensable as a source of moral instruction and guidance. How are we to live as Christians? We are to read the Bible and do what it says.

Thirdly, *Christian freedom does not mean selfish individualism.* 'Rather, serve one another in love.' There is a remarkable reversal in Paul's use of vocabulary here, for the verb 'to serve' is more literally 'to be enslaved to'. What a paradox, then! Paul waxes eloquent about freedom, and in the very next breath tells us to accept voluntary bondage!

Herein lies another difference between Caligula's freedom and Paul's. That Roman emperor's caprice was utterly selfish and individualistic. He claimed to be 'the one free man in the empire'. Well, of course, he was. His freedom was ruthless and unscrupulous, and it disfranchized everybody else. It was the freedom of a despot. Had Caligula been writing Galatians 5:13, it would have read: 'Use your freedom to indulge the sinful nature, and in hate make slaves of everyone.' For Paul, such egocentric licence was not true freedom at all.

Luther expresses the matter with his characteristic love of paradox in a famous book entitled *The Freedom of a Christian*. 'A Christian is a perfectly free lord of all, subject to none. A Christian is a perfectly dutiful servant of all, subject to all.' We do not understand what Paul means by freedom unless we have learned to hold those two propositions in tension.

Think of it this way. There are three types of dog on the city streets. The first spends his days chained to a post, whining and barking because he wants to be free of his master's control. Is he a happy dog?

The second wanders the streets, owned by nobody. A law to himself, he spends his days rummaging in dustbins. Is he a happy dog?

The third walks at his master's side. There is no lead, yet he rarely strays far, and always obeys his master's call. Is he a happy dog? I think he is!

Similarly, there are three kinds of people in this world. One type is strictly moral and respectable. These people never do anything that might imperil their high opinion of themselves. But those moral chains that restrain their actions are resented deep down. They are perceived as having been imposed by society or by a religious upbringing. If the truth were known, they would much rather break free from them. Their morality is a burden to them. Are they happy? No. Nomists are never happy people!

The second group of people have no moral inhibitions at all. They have embraced our late-twentieth-century permissiveness. They cheat, they lie, they sleep around. They think *Caligula* is a marvellous play, because what Caligula wants he gets. Are they happy? No. Libertines are never really happy people.

But there is a third kind of person. These people have discovered that obedience to the law of God is perfect liberty. They have learnt that the true self is encountered not through surrender to sin, but through voluntary surrender to God as their master, and in loving service of their neighbour. They have discovered that it is in these acts and attitudes that real fulfilment lies. Are they happy? I think you will find they are.

What the Spirit does
The battle inside

'Man is not truly one, but truly two.' Those are the words of Robert Louis Stevenson in another classic study of human depravity, *Dr Jekyll and Mr Hyde*.

Dr Jekyll is a respectable London doctor, kindly and religious. In the course of his scientific research, he discovers a drug which changes him into a repulsive and malevolent dwarf, whom he calls Hyde. In the person of Hyde he performs all kind of immoral and abominable acts. Yet Jekyll, for all his shame at these deeds, finds himself incorrigibly addicted to the experience of this *alter ego*. At one point he struggles for two months to abstain from the potion, yet finally weakens and takes it again, this time committing a brutal murder as a result. The more often he yields to the drug, the more difficult it becomes to regain his virtuous identity afterwards. Eventually the evil side of his personality so dominates him that he finds himself permanently wedded to the form and character of Hyde. In order to escape capture for his dreadful crimes, he commits suicide.

It is a fascinating book, more serious in its purpose than a mere horror story. It is a profound psychological analysis of moral conflict within a human personality. In some respects it anticipates Freud's discussion of the subconscious battle between the superego and the id. 'I have learned', says Jekyll, 'to recognize the thorough and primitive duality of man. Two motives contend in the field of my consciousness. Even if I could rightly be said to be neither, it is only because I am radically both. It is the curse of mankind that these incongruous faggots are thus bound together. In the agonized womb of existence, these polar twins are continuously struggling.'

Jekyll and Hyde are not to be thought of as bizarre characters in science fiction. Stevenson was painting a picture of us all. No matter how upright and charitable we may appear on the surface, there is, he says, a beast within, privately longing to surrender itself to all kinds of licentiousness. And the more often we indulge that beast, the less able we are to restrain its excesses by our will power. Whether we like it or not, we are all victims of this moral schizophrenia, this inner war.

That being so, don't you think Stevenson would find these verses from Galatians specially interesting? For here in Galatians 5 Paul too is describing an inner war; a war that in many respects mirrors that between Jekyll and Hyde.

Look first at the protagonists:

> The sinful nature desires what is contrary to the Spirit, and the Spirit what is contrary to the sinful nature. They are in conflict with each other, so that you do not do what you want (5:17).

Stevenson had a Scottish Puritan upbringing, and it is clear from some of his private letters that his familiarity with the writings of the apostle Paul did influence his story of Jekyll and Hyde. It would not be difficult to interpret the novel as a kind of allegorical commentary on this verse, with Jekyll's struggles against Hyde corresponding to what Paul calls the conflict between the Spirit and the sinful nature.

If Stevenson intended any such connection, however, he made a profound error. For there is an important difference between the struggle he depicts in his novel and the one Paul is talking about here. Stevenson is a pessimist. In the end Hyde masters Jekyll and destroys him. But for all his sympathy with Stevenson's realism about the inveteracy of evil and the doctrine of original sin, Paul emerges from this passage as an optimist!

Live by the Spirit, and you will not gratify the desires of the sinful nature (5:16).

That promise is expressed most emphatically. Paul is convinced that the conflict he is describing is one that issues in moral victory, not defeat. The story of Jekyll and Hyde is about an inner moral conflict that is common to all human beings. But Paul is not talking about the human race in general. His inner war is specific to Christian experience. That is the significance of his emphasis on the role of the Spirit. The 'spirit' he is referring to is not some higher moral self which all human beings possess, like Freud's superego. He is the Spirit of Christ — a divine person who dwells, according to the New Testament, exclusively in converted men and women.

Paul is not, of course, suggesting that Christians are the only people to experience inner moral conflicts. That would be nonsense! Everyone has a conscience. Everyone knows what it feels like to be tempted. Stevenson is right about that. But in non-Christians that moral conflict does not represent a collision between the Spirit and the sinful nature, for the simple reason that the Spirit isn't there. Rather, the non-Christian's inner war is generated by moral education. There is nothing supernatural about it. Parental discipline, social conventions, civil legislation, religious instruction – all these influences and authorities combine to cultivate in each of us an internal sense of right and wrong.

Paul has a word to embrace all those external authorities and influences that contribute to our moral education. He sums them up as 'law'. He knew from personal experience how savage an inner conflict the law could generate in a human personality. Back in chapter 3, he likened it to a gaoler. There could be no freedom for us while we were 'under the law', for it is in our human nature to rebel against such external moral constraints on our behaviour. And it is our fate to suffer the torment of guilt as a result.

The moral education which law provides is a social necessity in a fallen world, but there is no real hope in law. For the sad truth is that we human beings are sinful by nature. External moral influences and authorities, though they may partially condition our behaviour, can't eradicate that fundamental flaw in our moral make-up. Stevenson's novel describes the universal moral conflict which every human being experiences, especially those raised, like Stevenson himself, in morally minded families. That conflict is between internalized moral education on the one hand, and our innate moral corruption on the other. In that battle, the sinful nature does win. None of us, left to ourselves, has the power to live as our conscience dictates.

That is why Stevenson is a pessimist. And it is also why the nomists in Galatia had got it wrong. As Oscar Wilde says in that famous line from *Lady Windermere's Fan*: 'I couldn't help it. I can resist anything except temptation.'

External moral influence and authority, then, can educate our conscience, but they can never empower our wills. The law can condemn us, but it can never sanctify us. In the inner war between Jekyll and Hyde, Hyde is the final victor, and self-destruction is his final destiny. Stevenson is right: this is precisely the tragic plight of all men and women without Christ.

The Spirit on side

But Paul is not talking about men and women without Christ. He's talking about Christians! And within the consciousness of a Christian, a remarkable change has taken place.

If you are led by the Spirit, you are not under law (5:18).

The Christian is not battling to conform to some external moral standard from which he feels alienated. It is not a case of external moral education *versus* internal moral corruption. Christians have received a new nature. A supernatural guest has taken up residence within our personality: the Holy Spirit. And this divine presence not only informs our moral conscience, as the law did, but also empowers our moral will and transforms our moral character as the law never could. The arrival of the Spirit changes the whole balance of power in the inner war. It is no longer a case of Jekyll *versus* Hyde, but of Jekyll-plus-the-Spirit *versus* Hyde.

The Christian life is bound to be a war of inward moral tensions and conflicts. But it is not the old war. The old war was a losing battle, but this new war is one we can and finally shall win.

What are the signs of our progress in the campaign?

> The acts of the sinful nature are obvious: sexual immorality, impurity and debauchery; idolatry and witchcraft; hatred, discord, jealousy, fits of rage, selfish ambition, dissensions, factions and envy; drunkenness, orgies, and the like (5:19–21).

In some wars, it is difficult to tell who is winning. But this isn't one of them. Each side in the conflict Paul is talking about has a distinctive heraldry of its own, and there is no mistaking which flag is flying from the fortress of the soul at any one time. On the one hand, there are these acts of the sinful nature. Paul gives us fifteen examples of them; the list in not exhaustive. The words 'and the like' indicate that he could have enumerated plenty more, had he wished.

On the other hand there is the fruit of the Spirit:

> But the fruit of the Spirit is love, joy, peace, patience, kindness, goodness, faithfulness, gentleness and self-control. Against such things there is no law (5:22–23).

That final phrase means, I think, not simply that these virtues are not prohibited by the law of God (which would be a rather trivial observation), but that these inner qualities of heart and attitude do not belong to the realm of moral legislation. They are not the kind of behavioural norm you can command people to display. They are the product of inward moral renewal. They are the 'fruit' of the Spirit.

111

Now let me ask you a question. How much of this fruit of the Spirit have you got?

It is easy to be panicked by that question. We look anxiously down the list to see if it includes any qualities we think we have. 'Patience! Phew! Thank goodness! I am very patient.'

But that could be very deceptive. Notice the difference between these two phrases: 'the acts [plural] of the sinful nature' and 'the fruit [singular] of the Spirit'. That difference is significant. In any individual, only some of the acts of the sinful nature will normally be evident, for they are separable. Our moral weakness betrays itself in various ways. One person may be a generous drunkard, the other a selfish teetotaller. But any one of the acts of the sinful nature affords damning evidence of the moral corruption within us.

It is not like that, however, with the fruit of the Spirit. That fruit is given whole, not in pieces. So, for instance, the person who lacks self-control lacks the fruit of the Spirit, no matter how joyful he may be. And the person who lacks joy lacks the fruit of the Spirit, no matter how self-controlled she may be.

Some of us are naturally inclined towards one or more of these qualities which Paul lists. Patience, for example, is not an exclusively Christian virtue. Some people have a naturally patient temperament. The devil is not necessarily threatened by such isolated virtues. He can use them to tempt us to self-congratulation. He can exploit them in other ways too. For instance, he loves to make us so courteous and humble-minded that we finish up irritating one another. Or he takes a husband's determination to be faithful and twists it into hatred for the wife to whom he is 'shackled'. Such games are a great joke for him! When we want to assess the measure of the fruit of the Spirit in our lives, then, we must go to that quality in Paul's list that is *least* evident in our personalities, not the one which we like to think we display the most. There is an indivisible wholeness about this fruit, because it represents the rounded integrity of a Christlike character.

So I repeat my question: how much of this fruit do you have? This is important. Notice Paul's solemn warnings:

> I warn you, as I did before, that those who live like this will not inherit the kingdom of God (5:21).

> Do not be deceived: God cannot be mocked. A man reaps what he sows. The one who sows to please his sinful nature, from that nature will reap destruction; the one who sows to please the Spirit, from the Spirit will reap eternal life (6:7–8).

The moral quality of our lives, then, does matter. We cannot earn salvation by our moral obedience, but an absence of moral obedience puts a worrying question mark against our assurance of salvation. Paul urges us not to be taken in by people who tell us that because we are saved we can sin with impunity. It isn't so. People who live lives of gross sin will not go to heaven. Rather those who persistently invest in their sinful nature will reap a harvest of divine judgment. If our Christian testimony is to have any credibility, there must be moral evidence of the presence of the Spirit within us. How can we claim to be the children of God if there is no sign of the Spirit-generated family likeness?

In his *Confessions*, St Augustine tells us how at one point in his life he was moved to pray: 'Lord, give me chastity and self-restraint, but not yet. I will be holy shortly, in a little while. But my shortly grew into a greatly and my little while lengthened into a long while. For I didn't want my lust quenched, but rather glutted.'

It is perhaps a prayer with which we can easily sympathize. But Augustine was not a Christian when he prayed that prayer. Indeed, it is not a prayer a Christian ought to pray. There can be no assurance of salvation for anyone who is trying to delay the pursuit of holiness. To be a Christian is to have the Spirit of Jesus in our hearts. And that, at the very least, means beginning to demonstrate the fruit of the Spirit in our lives. Augustine could become a Christian only when he was willing to start praying, 'Lord, give me chastity and self-restraint, and give it now!' Holiness is not an optional extra. It is an urgent necessity, an indispensable evidence of the spiritual renewal which God has worked in us by his grace.

How then do we overcome the acts of the sinful nature? How do we produce the fruit of the Spirit?

What we must do

> Those who belong to Christ Jesus have crucified the sinful nature with its passions and desires. Since we live by the Spirit, let us keep in step with the Spirit (5:24– 25).

There are two mistakes Christians commonly make in regard to sanctification. The first consists in overemphasizing the role of human effort. That is the mistake of the nomists. Like the Galatians, having begun with the Spirit, they try to attain perfection through their own efforts.

114

And, as Paul has explained to us, those efforts are not enough. Dr Jekyll on his own must fail.

The second, and opposite, mistake is to underestimate the role of human effort. This error is sometimes called *quietism*. The quietists say you mustn't try to live a life that pleases God at all. You should just let it happen. They make much of Paul's statement that we have crucified the sinful nature. 'There!' they say. 'The sinful nature is dead. A truly spiritual person is immune to sin. Just as a corpse can't respond to a stimulus, so a Christian should be incapable of responding to temptation.' They often point too to the phrase 'led by the Spirit' (5:18), and interpret this to mean that Christians are to see themselves almost as Spirit-directed robots, doing the will of God without needing to think or decide or exercise their wills. To use an old catchphrase, the quietist says, 'Let go and let God.'

That is all very far from what Paul means here. If he were a quietist, we should hardly find him issuing moral imperatives such as: 'Each one should test his own actions' (6:4) and 'Let us not become weary in doing good' (6:9). The New Testament never suggests that our moral response to God should be passive. On the contrary, it describes the Christian life in terms of strenuous activity: 'Fight the good fight' (1 Timothy 6:12); 'Run . . . the race' (Hebrews 12:1); 'Make every effort' (2 Peter 1:5; Hebrews 12:14).

God's ideal Christian is not a remote-controlled zombie, but a new kind of human being: a self-determining individual who obeys God intelligently and serves him voluntarily (see Romans 12:1–3 and Ephesians 4:20–24). The difference between a Christian and a nomist is not that the nomist struggles and the Christian just 'lets go'. Rather, the nomist struggles in self-reliance and futility, whereas the Christian struggles in union with the Spirit and is therefore ultimately victorious.

Paul does not say that the advent of the Spirit brings our inner war to an end. Rather, it carries it to a new plane. D-Day has happened! The Allies have landed! Now we are marching to victory, instead of certain defeat. How then can we go on to the end of the march?

Steps to victory

First, *we must be decisively committed to Christ.* 'Those who belong to Christ Jesus have crucified the sinful nature with its passions and desires' (5:24). No way does Paul imply here that the Christian no longer has passions and desires. If that were true, where would be the inner conflict that he has been talking about? No, we still experience passions and desires. But we have made a decisive commitment to Christ, which includes a determination not to be mastered by those selfish drives.

Many have problems in their moral lives because they have never made such a decisive break with the past. Their repentance has been shallow, or even non-existent. They have never really severed their links with their sinful habits. In fact, they continue to fondle those habits.

Secondly, *we must daily align ourselves with the Spirit.* 'Keep in step with the Spirit,' says Paul (5:25). Notice the active verb. We are to walk in rank, like soldiers on parade, keeping in file behind the Spirit. This hardly suggests the remote-controlled movements of a robot or puppet. Paul makes his thought a little clearer in Romans 8:5: 'Those who live according to the sinful nature have their minds set on what that sinful nature desires; but those who live in accordance with the Spirit have their minds set on what the Spirit desires.' The focus of our effort, then, is our thinking. We are not to strive pedantically to obey rules, like the nomists. Neither are we to try to empty our minds and let God 'operate' us, like the quietists. Rather, God wants intelligent obedience. Our minds have been renewed by the Spirit, so we should focus them on the moral priorities of the Spirit.

A story from Greek mythology is often told to illustrate this point. There was a famous island inhabited by Sirens. Half-woman and half-bird, the Sirens beguiled passing sailors with their entrancing singing, and lured them to make shipwreck on the rocks. When the hero Odysseus passed by the island, he stopped his ears with wax and tied himself to the mast of his ship so that he could not be seduced. But when the Argonauts traced the same route, Orpheus employed a different strategy. He took a harp, and played music of such superior charm that the sailors gave no heed to the Siren song.

Paul seems to be advising a similar tactic in our moral battle with temptation. The Spirit stops immorality in us, not by saying negatively, as the law does, 'Thou shalt not commit adultery', but by generating in us the positive self-control necessary to practise chastity and marital fidelity. He puts an end to drunkenness in us, not by forbidding pleasure in a legalistic way, but by cultivating a more authentic joy that does not need the stimulus of alcoholic excess. He destroys self-centredness in our personal relationships, not by merely commanding us, as the law does, to 'love your neighbour as yourself', but by actually generating that love towards others in our hearts, together with the patience, kindness and gentleness that go with it. The Spirit's way is not to imprison Hyde in a straitjacket of rules, but to exorcise him with sweeter music.

Many fail because they relax the discipline of this daily alignment with the Spirit. They let the world, the flesh and the devil occupy their minds. And from there it is only a short step to falling out of line with the Spirit altogether.

> Let us not become weary in doing good, for at the proper time we will reap a harvest if we do not give up. Therefore, as we have opportunity, let us do good to all people, especially to those who belong to the family of believers (6:9–10).

If we are to be committed to Christ and aligned with the Spirit, we are, thirdly, *to be responsible for one another.*

> Brothers, if someone is caught in a sin, you who are spiritual should restore him gently. But watch yourself, or you also may be tempted. Carry each other's burdens, and in this way you will fulfil the law of Christ (6:1–2).

It's not unusual to find Christians who are rather negative about the church. But the church has a vital role to play in our moral progress. Notice the kind of social environment it ought to provide. It is not a competitive one, in which Christians keep trying to score holiness points off one another. 'If your church life gets like that,' Paul says in effect, 'far from helping one another, you'll just speed your common journey to hell' (see 5:15).

No, the social environment God demands is one of mutual caring. Notice also the moral discipline the church should exercise. There is an element of surprise in the word 'caught' (6:1). Paul isn't thinking of deliberate, persistent wrongdoing. He is talking about the kind of moral lapse which even otherwise godly Christians can experience, and which all too often becomes an excuse for sanctimonious gossip on the part of others in the fellowship. We are not to extract malicious satisfaction from our Christian brother's or sister's failures in that way. Rather, we must exercise a disciplinary care for them. The word 'restore' was used in the context of setting a fractured bone or repairing a piece of furniture. It implies that while we are not to ignore such moral lapses in the fellowship, and pretend they are none of our business, we are not to make capital out of them. We are to seek to heal people who fail, getting them back on their moral and spiritual feet again if we can. And we are to do this 'gently', that is, without censoriousness and belligerence. If rebuke is needed, it must be administered tenderly and without complacency. 'Watch yourself,' warns Paul, for it is a fallacy to think that any of us is immune to sin. Sometimes dealing with other people's failures will expose areas of moral vulnerability in our own lives, that we were not aware of. There must be no invidious comparisons.

If anyone thinks he is something when he is nothing, he deceives himself (6:3).

In the Greek original, the connecting word 'For' links this verse to the one preceding it. Paul seems to be saying that the chief reason we neglect this supportive role within the church is arrogance. We think we are too important to be bothered with failures. If they've got a problem, it's because, unlike us, they are weak. Like the Pharisee in the temple, we use the sins of others to bolster our own self-esteem. Nomism is often a first cousin to pride. But Paul warns us that we are not to spend our time making self-congratulatory comparisons with people in the church who have fallen.

Each one should test his own actions. Then he can take pride in himself, without comparing himself to somebody else, for each one should carry his own load (6:4–5).

There is no contradiction here with 6:2, 'Carry each other's burdens.' Paul is making a different point, namely, that we are ultimately accountable for our own lives and nobody else's. We must therefore evaluate our lives objectively by God's standards, not by self-inflated comparisons. We are to carry one another's burdens now, precisely so that we may be ready to carry our own burden on the day of judgment.

Note too the kind of ministry the church leadership should offer:

Anyone who receives instruction in the Word must share all good things with his instructor (6:6).

The primary job of the minister, then, is not to administer the sacraments, sit on committees, entertain visitors over a cup of tea, or run a taxi service for the infirm. The ministerial office is first and foremost for the purpose of 'instruction'. That teaching function rightly has a claim on the financial support of the fellowship. For nothing will help us to keep in step with the Spirit more than regular instruction from the Word of God.

A postscript

Those who want to make a good impression outwardly are trying to compel you to be circumcised. The only reason they do this is to avoid being persecuted for the cross of Christ. Not even those who are circumcised obey the law, yet they want you to be circumcised that they may boast about your flesh. May I never boast except in the cross of our Lord Jesus Christ, through which the world has been crucified to me, and I to the world. Neither circumcision nor uncircumcision means anything; what counts is a new creation. Peace and mercy to all who follow this rule, even to the Israel of God.

Finally, let no-one cause me trouble, for I bear on my body the marks of Jesus.

The grace of our Lord Jesus Christ be with your spirit, brothers. Amen (6:12–18).

In his final paragraphs Paul returns to the threat that prompted him to write his letter: the Judaizing false teachers and their campaign to promote circumcision. Why do they do it? Because they are legalists who think we must earn salvation by obeying the Jewish law? Because they are racialists who think the Jews are a spiritual élite and that we can find God's favour only by identifying with them? Because they are nomists who think the only way to overcome the power of sin in our lives is by keeping the Jewish law?

Yes, all these things were true of them. But Paul explains that underneath all those theological rationalizations there are two much simpler reasons for their enthusiasm for circumcision. First, they want to avoid being persecuted by their fellow Jews. Secondly, they want to be able to boast that they have won others over to their side.

'That', says Paul, 'is where I differ from them. I have no interest in ecclesiastical politics for its own sake. Christian ministry is no ego trip for me. There is only one thing that makes me proud, and that is the fact that Christ died on the cross for a wretch like me. That old self-obsessed religion I used to share with these Judaizers has been crucified with Christ. Circumcision and all the rest of that legalistic paraphernalia is a matter of total indifference to me now. For I realize that it all belongs to a world that is passing away. The future belongs to Christ and the new creation which he has inaugurated. The messianic peace for which the people of God have always yearned has arrived. But it will not be given to those who pursue a religion of law. It is for the true Israel of God, the children of Abraham who have faith in Christ. Let us have no more nonsense about circumcision, then. The only marks in my body that matter to me are the scars I have received as a faithful witness to Jesus Christ. And my only prayer as I bid you farewell is that his grace may be with your spirits.'

How to Trust God

GARY R MAYES

The hardest thing to do, when confronted with problems, confusion and chaos is – nothing.

Yet Abraham, David, Paul and many other experts in the art of living had to learn to do just that – to wait for God to act, to rest in the hope of his perfect timing, even when time had run out and God's intervention seemed impossible.

This book will help you to trust God, to wait for him and to commit your problems to him, especially when trusting, waiting and committing are the hardest things to do.

Gary R. Mayes is a graduate of Trinity Evangelical Divinity School, Deerfield, Illinois, and pastor of Faith Community Church in Santa Ana, California.

192 pages   *'B' format*

Crossway Books

A Sting in the Tail

ROY CLEMENTS

Take a fresh look at some of Jesus' lively and pointed tales from the Gospel of Luke. His parables speak to people of any age, culture and background as much today as they ever did.

Roy Clements deftly unravels these ancient stories. He avoids jargon, letting them shock, challenge and show us life as it should be.

160 pages   *Pocketbook*

Inter-Varsity Press